TEXAS

TEXAS BY ROAD

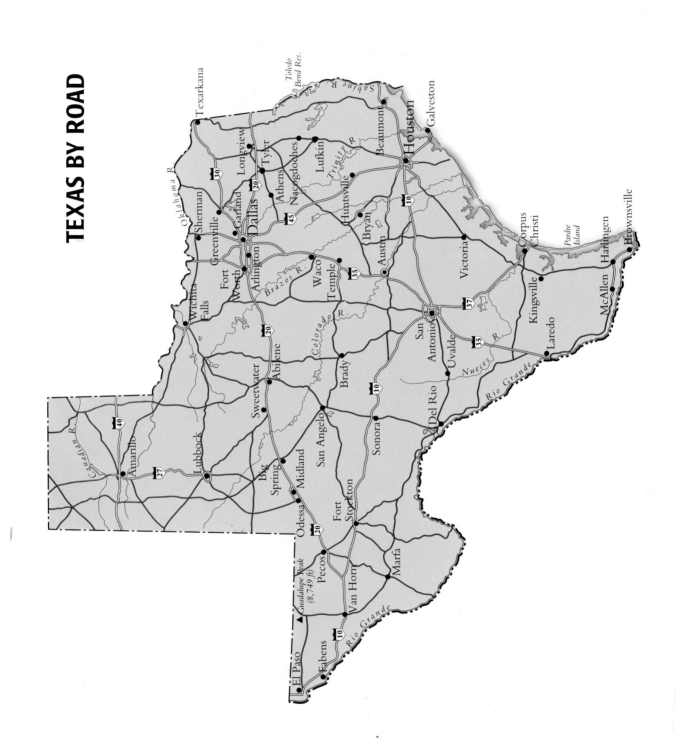

CELEBRATE THE STATES
TEXAS

Carmen Bredeson

BENCHMARK BOOKS

MARSHALL CAVENDISH
NEW YORK

To Dean and Lindsey,
my own Texans

Benchmark Books
Marshall Cavendish Corporation
99 White Plains Road
Tarrytown, New York 10591-9001

Library of Congress Cataloging-in-Publication Data
Bredeson, Carmen.
Texas / Bredeson
p.   cm. — (Celebrate the states)
Includes index.
Summary: Surveys the geography, history, people, and customs of the state of Texas
ISBN 0-7614-0109-1 (lib. bdg.)
1. Texas—Juvenile literature.   I. Title.   II. Series.
F386.3.B74 1997   976.4—dc20   96-11538   CIP   AC

Maps and graphics supplied by Oxford Cartographers, Oxford, England

Texas State Song, "Texas, Our Texas," Words by Gladys Yoakum Wright and William J. Marsh, Music by
William J. Marsh. Copyright © 1925 by William J. Marsh; Copyright renewed 1953 by William J. Marsh.
Reprinted by permission of Mary C. Hearne and Owen Edward Thomas, Copyright Owners; Publisher,
Southern Music Company.

Photo research by Matthew Dudley

Cover photo: *The Image Bank*, Michael Melford

The photographs in this book are used by permission and through the courtesy of: *Photo Researchers, Inc.* Jim
Grace, 6-7; Phillip Boyer, 13; Allen Green, 63; Garry D. McMichael, 66; Jules Bucher, 77. *Jim Olive/Stockyard
Photos:* 10-11, 14, 16, 51, 52 (left), 70, 71, 81, 82, 85, 127. *The Image Bank:* J. Brousseau, 17; Gary Russ, 24;
David W. Hamilton, 76; John Lewis Stage, 111; Michael Salas, back cover. *Texas Department of Transportation:*
Jack Lewis, 22, 118; John Suhrstedt, 26. *C. Allen Morgan/Peter Arnold, Inc.:* 27. Bob Daemmrich, 28, 48, 54-
55, 62, 67, 75. *The Witte Museum, San Antonio, Texas:* 30-31. *Corbis-Bettman:* 33, 89, 95. *State Preservation
Board of Texas:* 38, 41, 44, 45, 60. *North Fort Worth Historical Society:* 49. *UPI/Corbis-Bettmann:* 52 (right), 61,
91 (left), 102, 129, 130, 132 (top and bottom). *San Antonio Convention and Visitors Bureau:* Al Rendon, 72-73,
109; Texas Deptartment of Commerce, 79; Infomedia, 84; Richard Reynolds, 108; Dave G. Houser, 110.
Institute of Texas Culture: 86-87. *Manny Hernandez/Archive Photos:* 91 (right). *Austin History Center, Austin
Public Library:* 93 (PICA18956), 128 (PICA05491). *Reuters/Corbis-Bettmann:* 98, 99, 100, 131, 134. *Austin
Convention and Visitors Bureau:* Richard Reynolds, 104-105. *Karen Marks/Bat Conservation International:* 107.
Animals Animals: William Luce, 121 (top); Marty Stouffer, 124. *Dallas Convention and Visitors Bureau:* 121.

Printed in Italy

1   3   5   6   4   2

CONTENTS

TEXAS IS....

Texas Is . . .

" . . . a blend of valor and swagger."   —Carl Sandburg, poet

"Texas is a state of mind. Texas is an obsession. Above all, Texas is a nation in every sense of the word."   —John Steinbeck, author

Texas has a colorful history.

"I am about to enter Texas—my spirits are good and my heart is straight."   —Sam Houston, 1832

"I shall never surrender or retreat."
                              —William Barrett Travis, the Alamo, 1836

Texas is the land . . .

"It is impossible to exaggerate the pleasant character, the beauty, and the fertility of the province of Tejas [Spanish for Texas]."
                              —Father Antonio Olivares, 1716

"I must say as to what I have seen of Texas, it is the garden spot of the world, the best land and the best prospects for health I ever saw." —Davy Crockett

"Texas is too big a state to take in one gulp." —Texas *Monthly Guidebook*

. . . and the people who live there.

"I think Texans have more fun than the rest of the world."
—Broadway choreographer and Wichita Falls native Tommy Tune

"Nor is it a habit of Texans to look back. We have a tradition of looking forward and not looking back to see where we have been or who is following us." —President Lyndon Johnson

"What Texans can dream, Texans can do."
—Texas Governor George W. Bush

Texas is many things, but above all, it is home to the eighteen million residents who live within its borders. Texans come from all corners of the globe, and each has something to contribute to the place they call home. Let's take a look at the state of Texas and at the people who make it a great place to live.

1 THE MARKS OF TIME

Many things have left their mark on the place that we now call Texas. Millions of years ago, a shallow sea covered the land. Over time, plant and animal life from the prehistoric waters built up on the seafloor, leaving behind the raw material that became oil. When ancient volcanos erupted, the lava and ash that spewed forth helped to build the hills and mountains of west Texas. And, in their rush to the sea, roaring rivers gouged canyons and valleys out of the soil, creating some of the most spectacular scenery in Texas.

It was in those canyons and valleys that dinosaurs once roamed the land, searching for food to satisify their huge appetites. Some of them left the marks of their enormous feet behind, preserved in the limestone riverbeds of central Texas. Today, the dinosaurs have disappeared, but other interesting plant and animal life abounds in the wide variety of regions that make up the great state of Texas.

COASTAL PLAINS

Just inland from the Gulf Coast, low-lying salt marshes are home to many species of birds and insects. Endangered whooping cranes, whose wingspread can reach 7.5 feet, spend their winters in the Aransas National Wildlife Refuge. Their name comes from the whooping sound the birds make with their long windpipes.

The majestic whooping crane is among the rarest birds in the world. "Whoopers" mate for life and are famous for their elaborate courtship ritual filled with calling, flapping, and head bowing.

Naturalist John Audubon said he could "hear the whooper's call from three miles away."

Moving west, the land in the southern coastal plain is dotted with cactus, short grasses, and mesquite trees. Fruit from the prickly pear cactus, which tastes like kiwifruit, was a major food source for Native Americans. Today, the arid land is home to many cattle ranches. The most famous is the King Ranch, which is larger than the state of Rhode Island, and home to 50,000 head of cattle.

Under the thorny cactus and prairie grasses of south Texas, rattlesnakes slither into sandy holes. Coyotes roam the open spaces where few people live and howl at the moon on clear nights. The horned lizard can be found darting among the underbrush, feasting

Cowboys on a cattle drive. In the dry, dusty fields of Texas, cattle find water wherever they can and will often chew right through the thorns of the prickly pear cactus to get a drink.

on its favorite meal of red ants. These small creatures, which look like minidinosaurs, can squirt blood from their eyes as far as four feet, but no one knows why.

Deep in south Texas along the Rio Grande, which is Spanish for "big river," fruit trees and vegetables grow in the rich, river-bottom soil. Acres of grapefruit and orange trees sway in the breeze, while tomatoes ripen in the hot afternoon sun that shines down on the Rio Grande valley.

The northern region of the coastal plain is very different from the southern region. Land that was once home to only a few Native Americans is now filled with buildings, freeways, and cars. Race-car driver A. J. Foyt once said: "I feel safer on a racetrack than I do on Houston's freeways." Nearly one-half of all the people in Texas live and work in the large cities of the coastal plain. Industrial and automobile pollution in the urban sprawls of Houston, Dallas, and Fort Worth have created a smog-filled atmosphere that hangs over east Texas during much of the year.

Outside the cities, wilderness once again claims the land. Alligators swim in the bayous, and armadillos root around the Piney Woods in search of lizards and earthworms to eat. Early in the century, lumber companies cut down large sections of the pine forest. In order to protect what was left of the area, the 130-square-mile Big Thicket National Preserve was established in 1974. Here, trees and wildlife are safe to grow in a mild climate that produces nearly sixty inches of rain a year.

Occasionally, dangerous storms called hurricanes form in the Gulf of Mexico and take aim at the Texas coast. The word *hurricane* comes from the Mayans' word for their storm god, Huraken. The

A maze of freeways leads into Houston, the biggest city in Texas.

high winds, rain, and tornadoes that accompany the storms often destroy property and cause loss of life. During the hurricane season, which lasts from June until November, Texas residents who live along the coast must pay careful attention to the weather reports.

CENTRAL PLAINS

Huge herds of buffalo once roamed the treeless prairies and rolling hills of the central plains. In 1842, Texas rancher George Kendall said: "I have stood upon a high roll of the prairies, with neither tree nor bush to obstruct the vision in any direction, and seen these

STATE FAIR

For three weeks each October, Dallas is the site of the Texas State Fair. At the 277-acre Fair Park, visitors are greeted by a fifty-two-foot-tall talking statue called Big Tex. Once inside, the fairgrounds are full of rides and games, while booths display handmade quilts and home-baked pies. A livestock show and rodeo draws thousands who marvel at the size of the championship steer and watch nervously as bull and bronco riders hang on for dear life. The longest and best rides on the horses and bulls earn the most points for the contestants.

The State Fair draws more than three million visitors annually. During the rest of the year, the park is home to permanent exhibits. The Age of Steam Museum traces the history of American railroads. The Museum of Natural History has a 75-million-year-old mosasaur skeleton, found near Dallas. In the Dallas Aquarium, more than 300 species of fish, reptiles, and amphibians swim and crawl in their large tanks.

THE GALVESTON FLOOD

Early on September 8, 1900, a hurricane roaring out of the West Indies with a wind velocity of 135 miles per hour struck Galveston. The winds blew steadily for eighteen hours, sending enormous waves from the Gulf of Mexico sweeping across the entire city, submerging it under as much as five feet of water. More than eight thousand buildings were destroyed or damaged; an estimated six thousand people were killed. This was the worst natural disaster ever to hit Texas.

might-y day?_____ Was-n't it a might y day,__ Great

God, that morn - ing when the storm winds swept the town.

There was a seawall there in Galveston,
To keep the waters down;
But the high tide from the ocean, God,
Put water into the town.   *Chorus*

The waters, like some river,
Came rushing to and fro;
Seen my father drowning, God,
I watched my mother go.   *Chorus*

Well, the trumpets gave them warning
You'd better leave this place;
But they never meant to leave their homes
Till death was in their face.   *Chorus*

The sea began to rollin',
The ships they could not land,
Heard a captain crying, "God,
Please save this drowning man!"   *Chorus*

animals grazing upon the plain and darkening it at every point."

After hunters had killed off most of the buffalo, ranchers found the deserted land perfect for grazing large herds of animals. There are still nearly one hundred million acres of Texas that are considered "range" land. Today, thousands of miles of barbed wire fences enclose large ranches. Winters can be cold as wind blows across the flat land from the north. Heat returns to the area, though, during hot summers in this semiarid region.

GREAT PLAINS

To the west and southwest of the central plains are the great plains of Texas. The region begins in the far north, in an area called the Panhandle. This mostly flat land is barren, except for occasional trees and small shrubs. Tornadoes often swoop down from black clouds and snake across the plains, seeming to take aim at the area's small farms and ranches. Amarillo, the largest town in the Panhandle, is well known for its cold winter weather. An old saying goes: "The only thing between Amarillo and the North Pole is a barbed wire fence, and it's down."

South of Amarillo is the Palo Duro Canyon. Some of the cliffs that surround the canyon are one thousand feet high. On their craggy walls visitors can see evidence of several geologic periods. The red shale and mudstone of the lowest levels show that the area was once covered by a sea. The next level reveals that a swamp formed over the land as the water began to recede. Bones excavated from the ground in recent times reveal that a twelve-foot-long crocodile-like creature lived in the murky waters of the ancient swamp.

LAND AND WATER

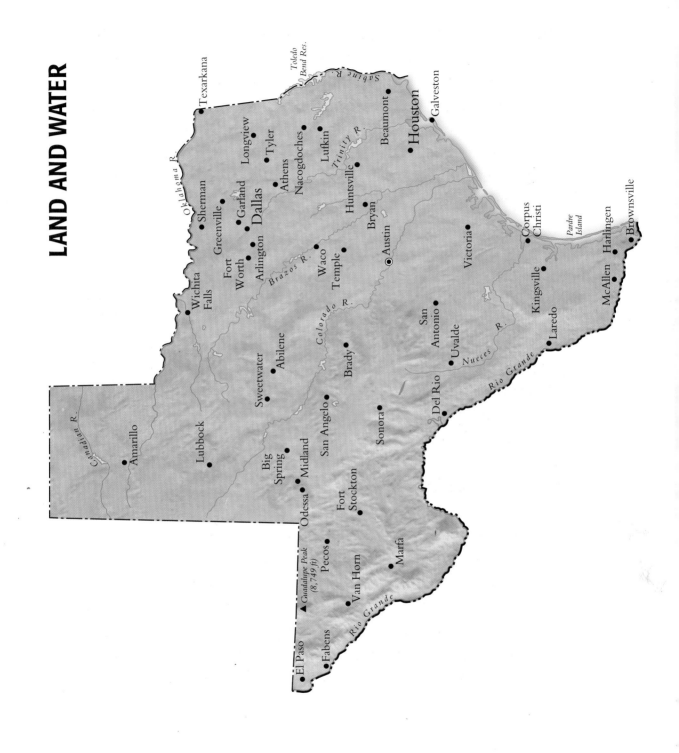

Lighthouse Rock in Palo Duro Canyon State Park comes as a surprise after mile upon mile of dusty, flat plains.

MOUNTAINS AND BASINS

Deserts make up much of the land in west Texas. Only cactus, mesquite trees, and small bushes grow on the parched land known as the Trans Pecos. Wood rats scurry along the ground, trying to avoid the snakes that wait quietly to strike. Mountain lions come out of the nearby hills to prey on the deer that inhabit the region. The mountains are part of the Rocky Mountain chain that extends all the way from Canada to Mexico, along the western United States.

The Rio Grande forms a natural boundary between Texas and Mexico. Canyons that were cut by the rushing river in prehistoric times have walls that rise to 1,500 feet above the water in some places. Giant petrosaurs once soared over the area. With their thirty-six-foot wingspan, they cast huge shadows on the hills and valleys below. Along part of the river is Big Bend National Park. Within the protected area, paisanos—better known as roadrunners—zoom along the dusty ground at speeds of up to twenty miles per hour.

All of west Texas is very dry, and a thin layer of white dust covers much of the land. High winds often blow across the desolate region and kick up large dust storms. In addition, the wind sends tumbleweeds careening across the landcape like huge bowling balls. When the plants blow into towns and across roads they can be dangerous, because some of them are the size of a compact car.

TEXAS WATER

Texas has hundreds of lakes and reservoirs within its borders. Most of them did not occur naturally but were created when dams were built along streams and rivers. These artificial bodies of water provide recreational areas where people can enjoy fishing and boating activities. They also serve as storage basins for water that is used by cities and farms.

The only large natural lake in Texas is Caddo Lake, located in east Texas. The Caddo Indians, who once lived in the region, believed that the lake was created by "powerful shaking earth

Chisos Mountains in Big Bend National Park

There is mystery everywhere, of the sun and the shadows on saw-toothed mountains, or mirages on the plain, of distance by day and stars bigger than walnuts, as near as they are far, by night.
—*from "A Tribute to the Southwest" by Dr. Walter Prescott Webb.*

spirits." In fact, it may have formed as a result of an earthquake that struck New Madrid, Missouri, in 1811. The effects of that huge quake created many new lakes in nearby regions.

In addition to its lakes, Texas has thousands of small streams and several major rivers. The most famous of them is the Rio Grande. It begins in the San Juan Mountains of Colorado, flows through New Mexico, and forms a 1,200-mile border between Texas and Mexico. Small communities dot the banks on both sides of the river. They are neither Mexican nor American, but a mixture of the two cultures.

In the northern part of the state, some of the border between Texas and Oklahoma is formed by the Red River, called Rio Rojo by the Spanish explorers. The river picks up particles of iron from the soil as it cuts through the Palo Duro Canyon. Those bits of iron give the water its reddish color. Explorers and pioneers often camped along the banks of the Red River during their journey to Texas. An old song, which was originally written about New York's Mohawk Valley, was adopted by westbound pioneers. The words were changed to fit the location. The song begins:

> Come and sit by my side if you love me,
> Do not hasten to bid me adieu,
> But remember the Red River Valley,
> And the one who has loved you so true.

HARMING THE LAND

Most of the rivers in Texas flow southeastward and empty into the Gulf of Mexico. Along the way, the waterways pick up pollution

A boat on the calm waters of Caddo Lake glides beneath hanging Spanish moss.

KEMP'S RIDLEY SEA TURTLES

By 1984, the smallest and most endangered of all the sea turtles was nearly extinct. During that year, only eight hundred nests were found at Rancho Nuevo, Mexico, the main nesting ground of the ridley sea turtles. In an effort to save the species, Mexico and the United States started programs to protect these turtles. In Mexico, the nesting grounds were guarded to keep animals and people away from the turtles, which weigh up to one hundred pounds, as they came ashore to lay their eggs. After the eggs were laid, they were carefully collected and taken to a fenced area of the beach, where they were put into protected nests.

When the eggs hatched, most of the little turtles were gently carried down to the beach and allowed to crawl across the sand and into the Gulf of Mexico. Two thousand of the silver-dollar-size turtles were not released, but instead were taken to Galveston to become part of a special program called Project Head Start. The hatchlings were put into saltwater tanks where they were fed and cared for during the next ten to twelve months by employees of the National Marine Fisheries Service. When they had reached the size of a Frisbee, the turtles were released into the Gulf of Mexico. Experts believed that their larger size would help the ridleys survive in the wild.

The Head Start program seems to have done some good. In 1995, there were 1,562 ridley nests counted at Rancho Nuevo, nearly twice as many as there had been eleven years before.

from the urban and rural areas. After heavy rains, some of the pesticides that farmers spray on their crops wash into the rivers. Industries located around cities also dump toxic waste into the water, along with sewage. Occasionally, thousands of fish are killed in Texas rivers as a result of the pollution.

Since many Texas rivers flow into the Gulf of Mexico, the bays and estuaries along the shoreline can also become polluted. High

Teenagers in Buchanan, Texas, help in an environmental study by testing the water quality of the Colorado River.

levels of mercury can be harmful to people who eat the fish, shrimp, and oysters of Galveston Bay. In the Gulf, oil spills and offshore drilling pollute the coastal region even more.

Texas wetlands are also in danger due to pollution and over-building. Efforts to save the wetlands and bays include educational programs for industry, ranchers, and farmers. Since 98 percent of Texas land is privately owned, conservation efforts can be tricky.

In order to educate students about the value of the wetlands, the Adopt-A-Wetland program was created by the Center for Coastal Studies. After a class selects a wetland to adopt, the students visit the site and learn about the plants and animals that live there. Other classes of older students collect more detailed information about the habitat and help conduct water quality tests. The program grew out of the simple question asked by a sixth-grade student: "How can we help save the wetlands?" Making young people aware of the importance of the wetlands is one way to help rescue them for future generations.

The enormous problems that we face with the environment will not be solved easily. It will take some personal sacrifice, along with new technology, to fix what is broken. Texans are accustomed to facing difficult situations and finding solutions, though. All you have to do is look at the state's colorful and sometimes bloody history for proof of the courage and determination of its people.

2 A COLORFUL PAST

Camp of the Lipans by Jean Louis Theodore Gentilz

When Spanish explorer Hernán Cortés conquered the mighty Aztec empire in 1521, he laid claim to a huge territory that included present-day Texas and Mexico. The Spanish government took control of the lands and sent settlers to colonize parts of the new empire. Those settlers met groups of Native Americans who had lived in the region for thousands of years before the Europeans ever set foot in the so-called New World.

THE FIRST TEXANS

Native Americans followed great herds of animals across the untamed lands of the North American continent. In time, a few groups of these wandering people, or nomads, migrated to the area that would one day be called Texas. Some discovered how to grow crops, and they settled in villages. Others continued to lead nomadic lives as hunter-gatherers, constantly searching for food to sustain their existence.

At the time of European contact in the early sixteenth century, several groups of Indians lived in Texas. Among them were the Karankawas, who roamed along the southern Gulf Coast. They wore little clothing and ate whatever they could find. Their diet included small game, wild plants, fish, insects, and snakes. They

Spanish conquistador Hernán Cortés entering Mexico territory.

often faced starvation because food was scarce in the barren coastal region.

The Apaches, who lived on the high plains of Texas, had a more reliable source of food. They traveled with large herds of buffalo and depended on them for many of their needs. Apache dwellings were built using the massive bones of the buffalo as supports. Some of the hides were draped around the framework to provide shelter, while others were made into blankets and clothing. Like the Karankawas, the Apaches lived in temporary camps and planted no crops.

Two groups of Indians in sixteenth century Texas lived in permanent villages and farmed. They were the Jumanos, whose camps were located along the Rio Grande in the southwest, and the Caddos of the eastern pine forests. Planting crops was one of the most important skills that these people learned. A dependable source of food allowed the nomads to stop their wandering and build more permanent dwellings. Growing crops such as corn, tomatoes, squash, and beans gave them some control over their futures. However, after the European explorers arrived, those futures were forever changed.

At the time of the first European contact, there were about 30,000 Native Americans in Texas. The Spaniards brought diseases to the New World, along with their horses and guns. The Indian populations had never been exposed to illnesses such as measles and smallpox, and entire villages were wiped out by devastating epidemics after the explorers arrived.

SPANISH MISSIONS

In an effort to settle the territory of Texas, the Spanish government and the Catholic church built several missions. The friars who ran the missions tried to convert the Indians to the Catholic religion and make them supporters of the Spanish government. Several communities were begun, including the Mission San Antonio de

CADDO CREATION LEGEND

The Caddo Indians of east Texas believed that a supreme being created the universe and controlled all within it. According to their legend, this god came into existence in the following way:

> In the beginning there was a woman who had two daughters, and one of them was expecting a child. One day the daughters were attacked by an evil monster and the pregnant woman was killed. The second daughter escaped and fled to tell her mother of the terrible tragedy. Mother and daughter returned to the site of the attack to find a drop of the slain girl's blood in an acorn shell. The mother took the acorn home, put it in a safe place, and covered it. During the night, sounds were heard coming from the shell. By morning, the drop of blood had turned into a tiny boy the size of a finger. Once again, the mother covered the acorn shell when night fell. By the next morning, the tiny boy had grown to the size of a man. He armed himself and went forth to slay the monster. The man returned home victorious and rose to the sky with his grandmother and aunt. From there he ruled the world.

Valero, which was established in 1718 and later came to be known as the Alamo.

A total of five missions were built in the San Antonio area. Each mission had a plaza in the center, surrounded by homes for the Indians and missionaries. Within the compound, there were workshops for weaving, tanning hides, and blacksmithing. In addition, reading, writing, cooking, and farming skills were taught to the native people. By the 1750s, more than two hundred Indians

CABEZA DE VACA

On a cold November day in 1528, a giant wave struck several small boats and threw men and supplies into the raging sea near present-day Galveston Island. One by one, eighty half-drowned Spanish explorers washed up on the sandy beach. Álvar Cabeza de Vaca, a member of the expedition, later wrote: "The survivors escaped as naked as they were born, with the loss of everything . . . " Karankawas rescued the men from the cold and took them to a nearby village. During the following winter, all except fifteen of the Spaniards died. Cabeza de Vaca was separated from the other survivors and spent several years living as a slave of the Karankawas.

In 1530, Cabeza de Vaca escaped and made his way to the forests of east Texas, where he became a trader among the Caddoan people. He later traveled south, where he met the only three of his shipmates who were still alive. The four Spaniards became well known as healers and medicine men after Cabeza de Vaca used a knife to successfully cut an arrowhead from deep in the chest of a wounded Indian. He wrote: "With a knife I carried, I opened the breast to the place, and saw the point was aslant and troublesome to take out. I continued to cut, and, putting in the point of the knife, at last with great difficulty I drew the head forth."

After the wounded man recovered, the Spaniards continued their journey across Texas. They were joined along the way by large groups of local people who had heard of their powers. In 1536, the men finally arrived at a Spanish settlement in northern Mexico and were reunited with their countrymen. Cabeza de Vaca returned to Spain in 1537 and wrote a book about the eight incredible years he spent living among the Native American people in Texas. The journal, called *The Narrative of Álvar Núñez Cabeza de Vaca*, was published in 1542.

lived in each of the five San Antonio area missions. That number steadily declined during the next several decades though, due mainly to disease.

By the end of the eighteenth century, there were very few Native Americans left in the missions, and the communities were abandoned in the 1790s. Spain then developed a new plan to colonize Texas. The government offered free land to United States and European citizens who were willing to immigrate to the territory. Many were interested in the offer of free land, but before any plans could be finalized, a revolution took place in Mexico.

UNDER MEXICAN RULE

For three hundred years, the European nation of Spain had governed the people of Mexico. By the 1800s, few Mexicans had any real ties to Spain, and most wanted independence from their distant ruler. Instead of engaging in war, the two sides met in 1821 and agreed to form the Republic of Mexico. Texas then became a Mexican state and was bound by the laws of the new Mexican government.

The government of the Republic of Mexico also decided to offer free land to colonists from the United States. Stephen F. Austin got a parcel of land from the Mexican government and established the first permanent Anglo settlement in Texas in 1821. He brought three hundred families to a site located between the Brazos and Colorado rivers and named his colony San Felipe de Austin.

During 1822 and 1823, the colony got off to a rough start. Most of the crops died during a long dry spell, and Karankawas raided

The Settlement of Stephen F. Austin's Colony, *by Baron de Bastrop, shows Austin reaching for a rifle as a wounded scout bursts in with word of an Indian raid on San Felipe.*

the area and killed many of the settlers. Some of the remaining families packed up and left, but others stayed. Conditions gradually got better at San Felipe de Austin when the hostile Indians were driven away and the drought ended.

In 1824, Mexico expanded its colonization laws to allow others to enter Texas. Thousands of immigrants flooded into the territory to claim property. Entire families traveled to Texas in loaded wagons. Spring rains often turned the desolate trails into rivers of mud. During the rest of the year, water was scarce and dust filled the dry air. Illness claimed the lives of many pioneers during their difficult trek into Texas. One young boy was found crying beside a wagon that was stopped in the wilderness. When asked what was wrong, he replied: "Fire and damnation, stranger! Don't you see mammy there shaking with the ager! Daddy's gone a-fishing! Every one of the horses is loose! There's no meal in the wagon!"

TO ARMS!

Although the colonists who traveled to Texas suffered hardships, they continued to pour into the state. Small towns grew, along with large ranches and cotton plantations. By 1830, the twenty thousand immigrants in Texas greatly outnumbered the Spanish-speaking residents. This alarmed Mexican officials, who decided to let no more American immigrants into Texas. Tensions between the settlers and Mexicans grew steadily worse. Many Texans wanted to be free from Mexican rule so they could establish their own government. With each passing year, more and more Texans volunteered to arm themselves and fight for freedom.

The first shots in the Texas war for independence were fired at Gonzales on October 2, 1835, when Mexican troops tried to capture a cannon from the Texans. The Texans, waving a flag that said "Come and Take It," fired on the Mexicans and drove them away. Riders were sent out into the territory on horseback to deliver signs that read:

Freemen of Texas
TO ARMS!!! TO ARMS!!!
Now's the day, and now's the hour!

Determined to halt the Texan rebellion, Mexican president Antonio López de Santa Anna amassed an army of four thousand soldiers. Santa Anna was an arrogant dictator who was described by one of his own officers as "a man drunk with ambition." The general traveled with a personal supply of silver and china, while his men went without food and warm clothing. As the poorly equipped Mexicans made their way north early in 1836, a small group of Texan rebels that included Davy Crockett, Jim Bowie, and William Travis, were holed up in the Alamo waiting for Santa Anna and his army.

REMEMBER THE ALAMO!

The Mexican troops arrived in San Antonio de Bexar on February 23, 1836, and surrounded the Alamo and its 189 defenders. For twelve days and nights they bombarded the old mission with cannon and rifle fire. Then, before dawn on March 6, 1836 (the 13th day of the siege), the Mexican army marched toward the Alamo from four directions and launched a full-scale attack. Soon, Santa Anna's men were swarming over the old stone walls and pouring into the Alamo courtyards.

Texan soldier Almeron Dickinson ran to his wife, who was hiding in the Alamo chapel with their fifteen-month-old daughter. He yelled: "Great God Sue, the Mexicans are inside our walls! All is lost! If they spare you, save my child." Fierce hand-to-hand combat took place within the dark, smoke-filled rooms of the chapel and long barracks, until the ground ran with rivers of blood.

In less than thirty minutes, all 189 Texans lay dead, along with

Siege of the Alamo
*Describing the plight of the besieged Alamo defenders, Colonel William Travis
sent out a message "To the People of Texas and all Americans in the World."
"I am determined to sustain myself as long as possible," he said, "and be
like a soldier who never forgets what is due to his own honor and that of his
country—Victory or Death."*

600 Mexicans. Fifteen women and children, including Susanna and
Angelina Dickinson, were found hiding in the chapel and were set
free by General Santa Anna. Hundreds of wounded Mexican
soldiers died in the weeks following the battle because there were
no doctors to treat their wounds.

Three weeks after the bloody Battle of the Alamo, Santa Anna's troops captured Texan colonel James Fannin and nearly four hundred of his men near Goliad. They were imprisoned for a week before they were marched out of town and executed by Mexican soldiers. News of the massacres at the Alamo and Goliad quickly spread, and many angry men left their farms and families to avenge the deaths of their fellow Texans. Their rallying cry became "Remember the Alamo! Remember Goliad!"

REPUBLIC OF TEXAS

Just four days before the Alamo fell, fifty-nine delegates met at Washington-on-the-Brazos to draft a constitution and declare Texas independence. General Sam Houston was given the job of commander in chief of the Texan forces. The six-foot-three-inch former governor of Tennessee was a colorful character who had lived with the Cherokee Indians.

After several weeks in the territory, General Houston gathered together a group of nine hundred men who were ready to fight for Texas independence. With Santa Anna hot on their trail, the small Texan army retreated and retreated until they reached a wooded spot on the San Jacinto River, where they set up camp. Santa Anna's army arrived a few hours later and camped just over a small hill.

BATTLE OF SAN JACINTO

All through the night, the Mexicans prepared for a dawn attack by the Texans. When the attack did not come by the next afternoon,

Santa Anna allowed his 1,200 men to sleep. He had so little respect for the Texan army that he even called in the sentries that stood guard around the camp. At about four-thirty, the quiet afternoon air was split by the sound of cannon fire. Sleepy Mexican soldiers groped for their weapons as Texans streamed into their camp screaming, "Remember the Alamo! Remember Goliad!"

The actual Battle of San Jacinto lasted only twenty minutes, but the killing went on for hours as the Texans sought revenge for their slain comrades. Many Mexicans threw down their weapons and jumped into a nearby lake yelling "Me no Alamo—Me no Goliad." On the banks, frenzied Texans fired on Santa Anna's men until the water turned red with the blood of fallen soldiers. As Sam Houston rode among his troops and tried to stop the killing, he shouted: "Gentlemen, I applaud your bravery, but damn your manners."

When the slaughter finally stopped, more than six hundred of the Mexicans were dead, while only nine Texans had fallen. Nearly all of the escaped Mexicans were captured, including General Santa Anna, who was found hiding in the marsh wearing a private's uniform. With the victory at San Jacinto on April 21, 1836, Texas won its freedom from Mexican rule.

TEXAS BECOMES A STATE

Following the Battle of San Jacinto, a general election was held in 1836, and Sam Houston was voted the first president of the Republic of Texas. Texas remained an independent nation for nearly ten years before being admitted to the United States in 1845, as the twenty-eighth state in the union.

Attacking Texans crash the Mexican barricades in this panorama of the Battle of San Jacinto.

A year after Texas became a state, Mexican troops attacked U.S. Army soldiers along the Texas-Mexico border, and the United States declared war on Mexico. Several battles were fought before the United States captured Mexico City in 1847 and declared victory. The Treaty of Guadalupe Hidalgo was signed by the United States and Mexico in 1848. In this treaty, the United States gained land that is now California, Utah, and Nevada, along with most of New Mexico, Arizona, and parts of Wyoming and Colorado, as well as Texas. For the nearly one million square miles of land that became the American Southwest, Mexico was paid $15 million.

On March 2, 1861, at the beginning of the Civil War, Texas seceded from the Union to become a Confederate state. Many of the most prosperous farmers and ranchers in Texas were slave holders who did not want to see their workers set free. During the Civil War, Texas saw little action within its borders, but it contributed large amounts of cotton and ammunition to the rebel army, along with 60,000 soldiers.

In Surrender of Santa Anna, *by William Henry Huddle, Mexican general Santa Anna surrenders to General Sam Houston, who lies wounded beneath a tree. This 1886 painting hangs in the Texas Capitol in Austin.*

POPULATION GROWTH: 1850–1990

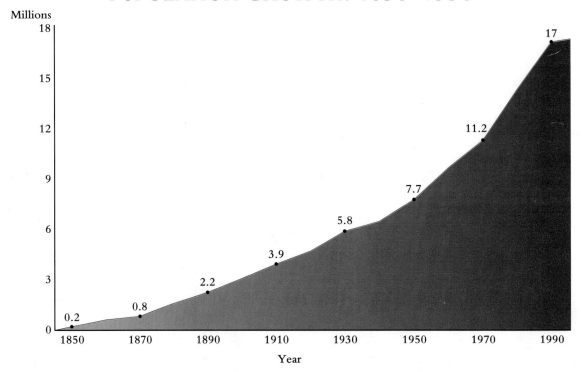

Millions

COWBOYS AND CATTLE

After the Civil War ended in 1865 and the slaves were freed, many of the large cotton plantations in Texas could no longer operate. As cotton production declined, a new industry took hold. Millions of head of wild longhorn cattle grazed on the state's huge expanses of range land. The horns on some of the rangy beasts measured eight feet from point to point.

Since the demand for beef was high in the rest of the country, Texas ranchers began to round up the wild cattle and move them

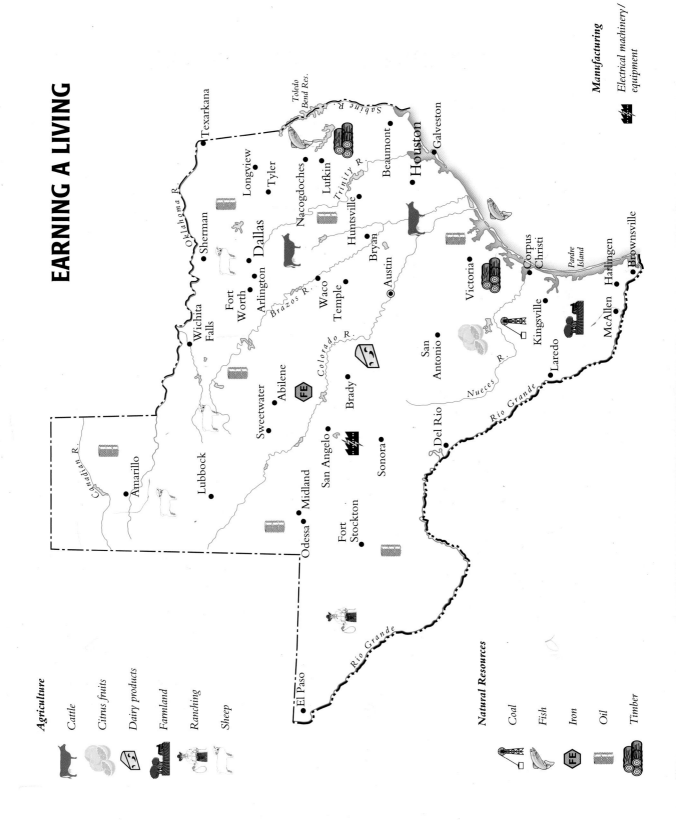

EARNING A LIVING

Agriculture

Cattle

Citrus fruits

Dairy products

Farmland

Ranching

Sheep

Natural Resources

Coal

Fish

Iron

Oil

Timber

Manufacturing

Electrical machinery/
equipment

El Paso

Amarillo

Canadian R.

Lubbock

Odessa

Midland

Fort
Stockton

San Angelo

Sonora

Del Rio

Rio Grande

Wichita
Falls

Sweetwater

Abilene

Brady

FE

Sherman

Fort
Worth

Arlington

Dallas

Waco

Temple

Brazos R.

Colorado R.

San
Antonio

Nueces R.

Laredo

Kingsville

McAllen

Harlingen

Brownsville

Padre
Island

Corpus
Christi

Victoria

Austin

Bryan

Huntsville

Trinity R.

Nacogdoches

Lufkin

Longview

Tyler

Texarkana

Oklahoma R.

Toledo
Bend Res.

Sabine R.

Beaumont

Houston

Galveston

Rio Grande

Rodeo star Bill Pickett. In 1903, he bit the upper lip of a steer in a trick that became known as "bulldogging." Pickett, "the Bull-Dogger," became a rodeo hero and helped glamorize the life of the cowboy.

The great cattle drives of the mid-1800s brought in the golden age of the Texas cowboy. The bond between Texas and its cattle is described in the poem "Cattle" by Berta Hart Nance:

> Other states were carved or born,
> Texas grew from hide and horn.
> Other soil is full of stones,
> Texans plow up cattle bones.

north in huge trail drives. The cowboys, who spent weeks on the trail riding herd over thousands of animals and camping under the stars at night, became the subjects of poems, songs, and legends. A poem called "Rain on the Range," by S. Omar Barker, paints a humorous picture of life on the trail. It begins like this:

> When your boots are full of water and your hat brim's all a-drip,
> And the rain makes little rivers dribblin' down your horse's hip,
> When every step your pony takes, it purt near bogs him down,
> It's then you git to thinkin' of them boys that work in town.

From 1867 until 1887, more than six million longhorns were moved from the Texas prairies to stockyards in Kansas and Missouri. From there, the cattle were loaded onto trains and taken to markets in the rest of the country. The great migrations stopped after thousands of miles of railroad track were laid in Texas during the 1880s. Once the trains were up and running, it was easier to move the cattle by rail.

The arrival of the railroads also brought more people to Texas; by 1900 there were three million residents in the state. The economy depended mostly on farming and ranching until 1901. That was the year when oil was discovered near Beaumont, Texas.

THE OIL STORY

In the water that covered Texas in ancient times, the skeletal remains of plants and animals piled up on the seafloor. Silt from rivers and surrounding land washed into the waters and covered the decaying matter. Layer after layer built up, while pressure from the mass generated heat. Chemical reactions took place over

This monument called Dedication to the Cowboy *is found in Pleasanton, known as the "birthplace of the cowboy."*

millions of years, and vast underground reservoirs of petroleum formed in the process. During the latter part of the nineteenth century, people began to develop drilling methods to reach some of the fossil fuel.

On January 10, 1901, an enormous explosion was heard as a column of oil belched from the ground under a drilling rig on Spindletop Hill, located near Beaumont, Texas. Until the monster well was capped nine days later, oil spewed out of the ground at a rate of one hundred thousand barrels a day. It was the biggest oil

When this fountain of oil surged from the ground at Spindletop, the "boom and bust" days of oil discovery had begun.

Texas has long led the country in oil production. The pay may be good, but a day on an oil rig means difficult and dirty work.

gusher the world had ever seen and marked the beginning of the huge petroleum industry that has dominated the economy of Texas ever since.

Hundreds of other wells were drilled in the area, and 17.5 million barrels of petroleum were pumped out of the hill in 1902. The United States became the world's largest producer of oil as a result of the Spindletop field. Dozens of future industry giants were formed during the frenzy that followed, including Gulf Oil, Texaco, and Mobil. As the Spindletop fields dried up, other huge reservoirs of oil were discovered all over the state. Refineries were built to process massive quantities of petroleum, and thousands of people were hired to work in the new industry. Almost overnight Texas went from an agricultural state to an industrial empire.

The arrival of the automobile guaranteed that the need for petroleum and gasoline would remain high. Trains, ships, and factories also began to convert their machinery to run on oil instead of coal. Oil burned much cleaner, took up less space, and required less man power than did coal. As the demand for oil rose, the Texas petroleum industry continued to grow and the state's population increased as more and more workers moved to Texas in search of jobs.

Other companies, which had nothing to do with oil, moved their corporate headquarters to Texas, lured by the warm weather and the healthy business climate. Houston, Dallas, and San Antonio became home to millions of people. Texas government had to expand along with the increasing population. Legislators from far-flung areas of the state were faced with the job of creating new programs and laws for all Texans, old and new alike.

3 POLITICIANS AND EVERYDAY PEOPLE

The Capitol in Austin

Laws and regulations affect the lives of Texans on every level. Mayors and city council members pass laws in local government. Counties are usually run by a judge and a commissioners court. The state operates under the direction of a governor, legislature, and the courts.

INSIDE GOVERNMENT

Texas government is divided into three branches: legislative, executive, and judicial.

Legislative. The job of the legislative body is to make laws for the people of Texas. Thirty-one members of the senate and 150 members of the house of representatives meet in session on odd-numbered years. They study matters such as the budget, education, and crime. The legislators decide how to best spend the money in the state treasury and discuss ways to make Texas a better place to live.

Proposals about things that need to be changed in the government are called bills. When a new bill is introduced in the house of representatives, the members talk about the good and bad points of the idea. After all of the debate is finished, each representative gets to vote on the bill. If more than half of the members vote yes,

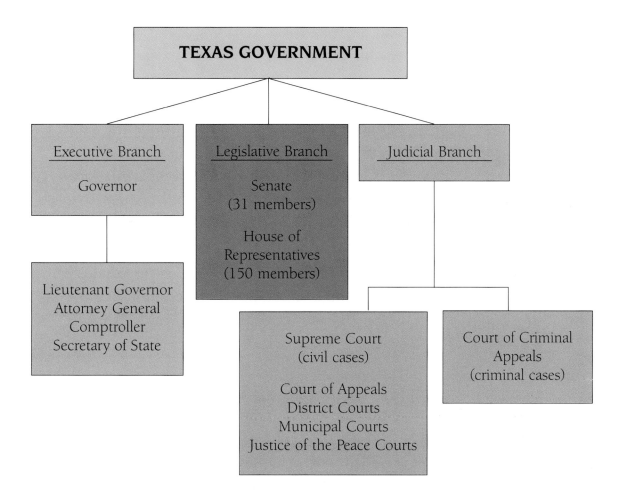

TEXAS GOVERNMENT

Executive Branch

Governor

Lieutenant Governor
Attorney General
Comptroller
Secretary of State

Legislative Branch

Senate
(31 members)

House of
Representatives
(150 members)

Judicial Branch

Supreme Court
(civil cases)

Court of Appeals
District Courts
Municipal Courts
Justice of the Peace Courts

Court of Criminal
Appeals
(criminal cases)

the bill passes. It then moves on to the senate, where it is also discussed and put up for a vote.

When a bill passes in the senate, it is then sent to the governor, who decides whether or not to sign it into law. If the governor does not agree with the proposal, he or she can veto the bill. After a veto, sometimes the legislature still wants the bill to become law. In that case, the members can override the governor's veto if two-thirds of them vote yes to the bill.

Executive. The governor of Texas is elected to a four-year term to head the executive branch. The governor prepares a budget for the state, makes sure that the laws are carried out, and represents Texas at various local, state, and national events. The governor also suggests topics for the legislature to study and signs bills into law.

Judicial. The laws of Texas are enforced by the judicial branch of the government. The state's highest court, the nine-member Texas Supreme Court, rules on cases involving a defendant's civil rights. Within each county and city there are also district courts that try local cases. When a defendant is found guilty of a criminal act in a lower court, he or she can ask the Texas Court of Criminal Appeals for the right to a new trial.

TEXAS POLITICIANS MAKE LIFE INTERESTING

What would Texas be without its colorful politicians? Sam Houston, the first president of the Republic of Texas, is probably the state's most famous political leader. After Texas became a state in 1845, Houston was elected to the United States Senate, where he served for fourteen years. In 1859, he became the governor of Texas and remained in that position until he resigned from office in 1861. Texas voters had chosen to secede from the Union during the Civil War, and Houston refused to swear an oath of allegiance to the Confederacy. Since the time of Sam Houston, many other Texans have entered the political arena, not only of Texas but of the nation.

Lyndon B. Johnson served as a United States representative and

TEXAS RANGERS

Early colonists in Texas were often attacked by hostile Indians, robbers, and bandits. To help protect the new landowners, Stephen F. Austin created "ranging companies" to guard the settlers. As the only real lawmen in Texas for many years, the rangers earned the reputation of being tough and effective. To qualify as a Texas Ranger, it was said that a man had to "ride like a Mexican, track like a Comanche, shoot like a Kentuckian and fight like the devil." Indeed, Mexican bandits called them "Los Tejanos Diablos," or the Texan devils.

In 1826, the Texas Rangers were officially organized. For decades they have been called in to assist local sheriffs and police in especially tough situations. Even though they are headquartered in Austin, there are six companies of rangers scattered throughout the state. They wear no uniforms, other than a white cowboy hat. Today, just over one hundred men and women wear the badge of a Texas Ranger. As part of the Texas Department of Public Safety, their jurisdiction covers the entire state and their presence is usually welcomed in tough criminal cases.

senator before becoming vice-president, and then president in 1963, after the assassination of President John F. Kennedy. Johnson was known for his hard work and long days at the office. He once said: "I seldom think of politics more than eighteen hours a day."

In 1966, Barbara Jordan became the first African-American woman elected to the Texas senate. Before the legislative session started, someone asked Jordan if she was scared. She replied: "I have a tremendous amount of faith in my own capacity. I know

Sam Houston. After visiting Sam and Margaret Houston in 1845, Harriet Virginia Scott described the president of the Republic of Texas as "decidedly the most splendid looking man I ever saw . . . walking up town with his Mexican blanket thrown over his shoulder, with an air of lordly superiority . . . intellect and nobility stamped on every feature you would declare that he was a man born to govern."

President Lyndon B. Johnson demonstrates his cattle-herding skill.

how to read and write and think, so I have no fear." After serving in the senate, Barbara Jordan became the first Texas woman elected to the United States House of Representatives.

Other Texans have gone far in the world of politics. Denison native Dwight Eisenhower served two terms as president, from 1952 until 1960. George Bush served for eight years as vice-president before being elected to the presidency in 1988. Bush was originally from Massachusetts but moved to Texas after World War II. Kay Bailey Hutchison of Dallas became the first Texas woman elected to the United States Senate. And Sandra Day O'Connor, born in El Paso, became the first woman ever appointed to the United States Supreme Court.

TOUGH ON CRIME

Texans tend to come on strong in their responses to crime. Like most states, Texas still has a great deal of criminal activity, but the adult crime rate in the state fell by nearly nine percent in 1993–94, and continues to fall today. However, juvenile arrests have been rising. Many factors play a role in teen crime, including an increase in runaways and gang activity in the state. In San Antonio, there were more than 1,000 drive-by shootings in 1993. Police officer George Sexton said: "People are afraid to go outside."

A police memorial service for officers killed in the line of duty. Texas has over forty thousand law enforcement officers, the third largest force in the United States.

In the shadow of the boom city of Houston, poverty is widespread among minorities. Many African Americans and Latinos suffer from unemployment and poor housing.

Teens who have run away from home often commit crimes in order to survive. In Houston, 1,500 homeless teens can be found on the streets on any given night. As many as 85 percent of them use drugs, and 25 percent of them are HIV-positive. One boy who was interviewed said: "Sometimes I just look to the future, and sometimes it's just like 'Is this it? Is this all there is?'"

Broken homes, poverty, and a lack of education all contribute to teen crime. Many young people band together to try and escape a horrible home life. In their search for a place to belong, some join gangs at a very young age. Instead of finding the security and protection that they so desperately need, these children often become involved in criminal activities. Fourteen-year-old Ralph, who joined a gang in the fifth grade, said: "I started running the streets and not coming home at night. It was all right for awhile, but it got to the point that it was too wild. When people start shooting at you, your family and friends, then you want to change."

In an effort to cut down the amount of crime committed by young people, many Texas cities now have teen curfews. In places such as Houston, Dallas, and San Antonio, those under age seventeen cannot be out in public between midnight and 6:00 A.M. Minors who are caught can be arrested, charged with a Class C misdemeanor, and fined $50 to $500. In addition, the 1995 Texas legislature passed a new law that allows juveniles to be tried as adults at age fourteen instead of fifteen in cases of capital murder and first-degree felony.

In a matter related to crime, the 1995 Texas legislature also passed a law that will give Texans over the age of twenty-one the right to carry a concealed weapon. In order to get a permit to carry a gun, a person must have no criminal record, pay a $140 application fee, and take at least fifteen hours of classes in gun use and safety. Texas is not alone in its response to a rise in violence. Thirty-eight other states have also enacted various laws that allow private citizens to carry guns.

SCHOOLS, WORK, AND WELFARE

Providing a good education for its young people is one of the best ways for a state to cut down on the crime rate. In 1995, Texas spent

$19 billion to educate the state's 3.5 million students. Teenagers who regularly attend school and learn job skills are less inclined to get involved in criminal activities. In order to make the schools better in Texas, the 1995 legislature passed sweeping reforms. In the future, many important decisions about the schools will be made at the local instead of the state level. Each district will be able to make its own rules, in partnership with the teachers and parents.

Welfare reform is another area that got a lot of attention in the 1995 Texas legislature. Laws were passed that limit the time during which people can collect welfare payments. In an attempt to assist people in getting off welfare, a new state agency was formed to help people learn skills and find jobs. Texas governor George W. Bush, son of the former president, said: "There's nothing more harmful than dependency on government. I have always felt that dependency on government saps the soul and drains the spirit."

In 1994, Texas led the nation in the number of new jobs created. Across the state, the unemployment rate was 6.4 percent for that year. For some areas, though, the jobless rate was much higher. In the Rio Grande valley, deep in south Texas, 17 percent of the residents could not find jobs. Many valley residents are migrant farmworkers who move from job to job, picking fruits and vegetables as the crops ripen in the fields.

There are nearly a million farmworkers who travel across the United States every year in search of work. At one farm, Valentina Lopez and her family had to live in a one-room shack that had no plumbing. She said: "There was just one mattress on the floor, and the roof leaked when it rained. And the rats. There were lots of them. The whole place smelled bad." She said that her children

Mexican workers harvest cabbage in the Rio Grande Valley.

cried and were afraid to stay there. The same story can be told for many other migrant workers, who must live in horrible conditions while they try to make enough money to feed their families.

IMMIGRATION

Many of the migrant farmworkers living in Texas are U.S. citizens; others have come into the United States illegally. Of the estimated 4.8 million illegal aliens in this country, nearly 400,000 live in Texas. Many of them are Mexican men and women searching for jobs as construction workers, gardeners, and maids. In their own country, the economy is in such bad shape that workers often make less than one dollar an hour.

In the United States, the minimum wage is $4.25 an hour and new legislation may raise it even higher. Even though undocumented immigrants often are not paid the minimum wage, they can

Mexicans pass through an opening in the border, seeking opportunity up north.

ILLEGAL IMMIGRATION

The issue of illegal immigration has sharply divided the citizens of Texas. A 1995 poll showed that 61 percent of Texans questioned wanted the state to pass legislation barring undocumented aliens from public schools, non-emergency health care, and social services. Those opposed to cutting off aid are troubled by the growing anti-immigrant sentiments. Marvin Andrade, who is president of his senior high school class, said: "What will happen to our cousins and families? Just because they don't have a little piece of paper does not mean they are less than us."

The issue becomes very confusing when illegal immigrants have children while living in the United States. Children who are born here are automatically American citizens and eligible to receive benefits. Should health care be granted to the child but denied to the parents? Education is another area of concern to many. If young illegal immigrants are barred from the public schools, they will never be able to rise above a life of poverty. Many Texans believe that it is in the best interest of the state to educate all of the children living within its borders.

As the economy in Mexico continues to decline, more and more illegal immigrants will enter Texas in search of a better life. The issue of how to best serve their needs without bankrupting the state treasury will continue to be the topic of debate for some time to come.

make a better living here. Problems arise, though, when the states have to provide education and health care for these people, who pay no taxes in this country. United States senator from Texas, Kay Bailey Hutchison, said: "Our schools, our hospitals, our social services and our prisons are being overwhelmed." Texas attorney general Dan Morales said that illegal immigrants cost Texas an estimated $1.3 billion in 1993.

There are those who would deny all services to the people who enter the United States illegally. They argue that if families cannot pay taxes and help support the government, they should not receive benefits. Others feel that since all Americans, except native peoples, are descendents of immigrants, we should do what we can to help give these recent arrivals a new start.

ECONOMIC POWERHOUSE

In spite of the high unemployment figures in the Rio Grande valley, Texas has a healthy economy. If Texas were still an independent

1995 GROSS STATE PRODUCT: $499 BILLION

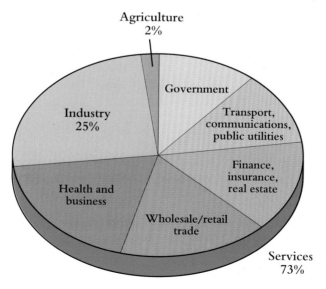

Agriculture
2%

Government

Industry
25%

Transport,
communications,
public utilities

Finance,
insurance,
real estate

Health and
business

Wholesale/retail
trade

Services
73%

country, it would have the eleventh largest economy in the world, ahead of Russia and Mexico. The state leads the nation in the production of oil, natural gas, cotton, and livestock. Texas produces a quarter of the crude oil found in this country and grows a third of the cotton. Manufacturing also provides jobs for millions of the state's residents, especially in large cities such as Dallas, Houston, and San Antonio, where refineries turn crude oil into gasoline and chemicals, while computer firms build ever more advanced electronic equipment.

Houston was transformed into a major port for international shipping when a canal was dredged to create a seaport far enough inland to be safe from hurricanes.

The Professional Rodeo Cowboys Association sanctions about 650 rodeos a year. In some parts of Texas, going to the rodeo is a more popular pastime than going to the movies.

Tourism is also big business in Texas. The state's 267,300 square miles of territory include beaches, mountains, cities, and parks. Millions of tourists spend more than $20 billion every year visiting interesting sites in the second largest state in the Union, after Alaska.

People from many different ethnic groups and nationalities live and work within the borders of Texas. Their talents and customs help to make the state an interesting place in which to live, as well as to visit.

4

A PATCHWORK OF CULTURES

Texas is like a great big patchwork quilt, where scraps have been stitched together to form a finished picture. The quilt tells a story of struggle and bloodshed, joy and hope. Within the borders of the quilt are pictures that represent all that is Texas. There is the cowboy, alone on the range with his longhorn cattle and his campfire. His image has helped define Texas in the eyes of the world. There are still many places in the Lone Star State where cowboys oversee huge herds of livestock. The cowboy of today, though, might use a jeep or helicopter to round up the animals, and call folks back at the ranch on a cellular phone.

THE SPANISH CONNECTION

Another piece of Texas that has cast an indelible picture on our minds is the mighty Rio Grande. Early Spanish explorers crossed the river into the land that would become Texas. Over time, they intermarried with the Native Americans and Mexicans to form a group that we know as Latino. As many as 25 percent of the people living in Texas today are of Latino origin.

Although the Rio Grande forms a barrier between Texas and Mexico, it has never been able to contain the culture of either area. In towns on both sides of the river, open-air markets display colorful

Sunday concertgoers relax in Travis Park, San Antonio.

piñatas and pottery, along with bright red bunches of chili peppers that are guaranteed to wake up the taste buds.

The influence of Latino culture does not stop in south Texas but extends into all parts of the state. Hungry Texans often order big, steaming plates of enchiladas and fajitas at their favorite restaurants. While they eat the spicy Mexican food, a group of mariachi might wander by and serenade the diners with a lively song, such as "Jarabe Tapatio," the Mexican Hat Dance.

Many Latinos make their homes in south Texas, especially in towns along the Rio Grande. Unemployment is high in the border towns, and there is a great deal of poverty in this region of Texas. Children often have to quit school to help support their families. As

THE CHILI PRAYER

"Lord God, You know us old cowhands is forgetful. Sometimes I can't even recollect what happened yestiddy. We is forgetful. . . . But I sure hope we don't ever forget to thank You before we is about to eat a mess of good chili." (Said by Bones Hooks, cowboy cook)

Pedernales River Chili

4 pounds of ground beef
1 large onion, chopped
2 cloves of garlic, crushed
1 teaspoon of oregano
1 teaspoon of ground cumin seeds
6 teaspoons of chili powder
2 16-ounce cans of tomatoes
2 cups of hot water
salt and pepper to taste

Ask an adult to help you brown meat along with onions and garlic. Drain the grease. Add the rest of the ingredients and bring to a boil. Lower the heat and simmer for an hour, covered.

This chili was served on the ranch of former president Lyndon Johnson. Johnson once proposed that chili be made the state food of Texas.

The Cinco de Mayo festival celebrates Mexico's victory over France in the Battle of Puebla. San Antonio is strongly influenced by Mexican culture.

many as half of the state's Latino children are born into poverty and never graduate from high school.

Bilingual education is an important issue in Texas schools. While some people want to see only English spoken, others feel differently. They believe that a child can learn more easily when taught in his or her native tongue, and that English can come later. Teacher Linda Velasquez says: "The idea is to get them educated, not just to learn English."

THE EUROPEAN CONNECTION

As we leave the small border towns of south Texas, we see in our picture large, bustling cities full of freeways, factories, and skyscrapers. The millions of people who live in these cities are from a

ETHNIC TEXAS

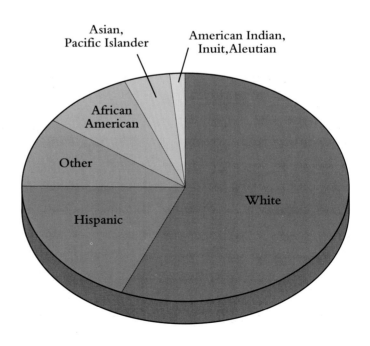

Children perform Flemish dances from their families' native land at the Texas Folklife Festival in San Antonio.

variety of racial and cultural backgrounds. The majority can trace their roots to European ancestors who helped settle the United States and Texas. Colonists from countries such as Germany, France, and England streamed into Texas to begin new lives in the 1800s. They brought along recipes, songs, and memories that have been woven together to help form the fabric of Texas.

When the German settlers arrived in America, they brought Christmas traditions from their native land. It was in Germany, hundreds of years ago, that people first used fir trees to decorate their homes at Christmas. German children also waited impatiently for a visit from St. Nikolaus, who left gifts under the tree.

TEXAS FOLKLIFE FESTIVAL

Each August, San Antonio is the site of a four-day festival that celebrates the different cultures in Texas. The sound of music and the smell of ethnic food fill the grounds that surround the Institute of Texan Cultures. Visitors can listen to a bluegrass banjo or a Scottish bagpipe while they eat Mexican frijoles (beans) or Irish boxty (potato pancakes).

As part of the entertainment, A. J. Judice and his friends hold crawfish races throughout the festival. Judice explained in his colorful Cajun dialect: "Louisiana crawfish, they be for eatin'. Texas crawfish, now they be for racin'. We want ever'one come by, watch the race, have fun with us. You wait, you'll see—don' take much for us Cajuns to have a real good time." The Cajuns, who are descended from French settlers in Louisiana, are well known for their music, humor, and spicy food.

Christmas in America might be very different today without the wonderful customs of the German people.

In the early days, the Germans continued to speak their native language, as did many other immigrants to Texas. With the passage of time, however, those languages were replaced with English. About three out of four Texans can trace their roots to European ancestors. These English-speaking people are often referred to as Anglos by the Latino population. During state fairs and festivals, many booths are filled with items like the ones that were brought to Texas by the settlers. Handmade quilts and wooden rocking chairs share space with fruit-filled kolaches and jars of peach preserves.

TRAGEDY

Today's Anglo Texans live in communities, large and small, all over the state. Some are still farmers and ranchers, while others work in urban businesses and industries. As busy Texans zoom along the freeways in the large cities, many rarely stop to examine what is just beyond their vision. It is along many of the freeways that small, worn-out houses crouch in the smog-filled shadows, where trash litters the streets and shots ring out in the darkness.

A young Houston Rockets basketball fan

Women have long played an active part in ranch life. In "Song of the Forerunners" poet Karle Wilson Baker describes the "women who bore Texas:"

Stern women, laughing women, women stout or small,
Bronzed women, broken women—brave women, all.

This part of the Texas quilt is not pretty, but it is the grim reality of what life holds for many of those who are too poor to escape to the suburbs. Just like in the rest of America, there are enormous problems in many Texas inner cities. The residents must live their lives surrounded by drugs, gangs, and poverty. Young people, who often live in single-parent homes, grow up feeling helpless and angry. Some join gangs and terrorize the frightened residents of the crime-filled neighborhoods. Black community leader Ernest

McMillan said: "We have gone from fearing the Klan [a white Supremacist group] to fearing our own children."

Many of the people living in the inner cities of Texas are African Americans, who account for about 15 percent of the state's population. They did not come to Texas willingly but were brought here to work as slaves, planting and harvesting huge cotton crops. It wasn't until June 19, 1865, at the end of the Civil War, that the 200,000 slaves in Texas were told of their freedom. That day, which is known as Juneteenth, is celebrated today in communities all across the state. During the festivities, families gather together to eat "down home" food such as corn bread and barbecue and to watch fireworks light up the night sky.

THE FIRST TEXANS

No picture of Texas would be complete without images of the state's first residents, the Native Americans. Thousands of years before the Europeans arrived, Indians lived and hunted in the wild and remote lands of present-day Texas. Today Indian culture can still be seen at two reservations in the state, located in east and west Texas. While some Indians continue to live on the reservations, most of the state's 65,000 Native Americans live in cities and towns, like other Texans.

Some of the Indians in Texas spend several weekends each year going to powwows in order to stay in touch with their heritage. At the festivals, there are demonstrations of native dances and smoke signal displays. While native drums beat in the background, visitors can sample traditional Indian foods, such as mesquite bread, and buy baskets and pottery at the many booths that circle the powwow area. Ken Brown works in a library during the week and enters war dance contests on the weekends in authentic feathered costume. "We celebrate our culture every weekend in a wholesome family environment," he says.

Children learn about the daily lives of Native Americans at the Institute of Texan Cultures in San Antonio. From Spanish colonists to Indian tribes and Dutch dairy farmers, the institute represents every nationality and cultural group that has shaped Texan history.

Asian newcomers embrace the traditions of Texas. Nearly 500,000 Asian Americans now live in Texas.

NEW FACES

In spite of the mountain of images created by the state's various groups, the Texas quilt will never really be finished. Each year brings new residents to the state from countries such as Vietnam, India, and Haiti. Along with them come traditions that gradually seep into the patterns of our lives. Texas is an ever-changing picture. There is one thing that remains the same, though, and that is the determined spirit of the people of Texas. That spirit is the common thread that runs through the history of our state and makes the fabric of Texas strong.

5 TALENTED TEXANS

Houston art collector Dominique de Menil once said: "Man cannot live by bread alone. We need painters, poets, musicians, filmmakers, philosophers, dancers and saints." There are many talented people living within the borders of Texas. Some entertain us with their music and words, while others amaze us with their artistic and athletic abilities.

MUSIC FOR EVERYONE

Texas has music to please almost any taste. For classical music fans, there are symphony orchestras and opera companies in all the major cities. Several musical festivals are also held every year, including the Van Cliburn International Piano Competition in Fort Worth, named for the state's most famous pianist.

Van Cliburn began to play the piano when he was a young child. When he started first grade, his teacher asked him if he could read. He answered: "Well, no, ma'am. I can't read writing, but I can read music." The Cliburn family had two pianos in the house and two more in the garage for the young prodigy to use.

In 1947, when Van Cliburn was just thirteen years old, he made his debut with the Houston Symphony Orchestra. One year later, he played in Carnegie Hall in New York City. Music critics marveled

Twenty-three-year-old Van Cliburn, after wild applause for his performance at the Tchaikovsky piano competition in Moscow, is personally congratulated by Soviet premier Nikita Khrushchev.

at his extraordinary skill. In 1958, Cliburn became the first American to win the Tchaikovsky Gold Medal in Moscow. At that time, Soviet premier Nikita Khrushchev looked up at the six-foot-four-inch pianist and asked: "Why are you so tall?" Van Cliburn answered: "Because I am from Texas."

For those whose musical tastes are less lofty, Texas has thousands of country-and-western bands. In many small-town honky-tonks on Saturday night, fans listen to the twang of a steel guitar and dance the Texas two-step. Where there is not a live band performing, fans play the records of their favorite country stars on the jukebox.

George Strait of Pearsall is certainly a jukebox favorite in Texas. A five-time winner of Country Music's Entertainer of the Year Award, Strait did not even learn to play the guitar until he was in the army. Since that time, the clean-cut singer in the pressed jeans and Resistol hat has recorded dozens of number one country hits.

Willie Nelson, with his braided hair, scruffy beard, and beat-up guitar, is another Texas favorite. He went to Nashville during the 1960s to be a songwriter. There he wrote classics such as "Crazy." After returning home in 1972, Nelson began to perform some of the songs that he had written. As the popularity of country music spread across the United States, so did Willie Nelson's fame.

Another type of music that attracts many fans in Texas is called Tejano, which combines rock, pop, and country with a Latin beat. One of the biggest Tejano stars was twenty-three-year-old Selena Quintanilla Perez, who received a Grammy Award in 1994 for her album, *Selena Live!* The popular Mexican-American performer was working on her first English-language album when she was murdered on March 31, 1995, in Corpus Christi.

Yolanda Saldivar, president of Selena's fan club, was charged with the murder and taken into custody. She was later tried for the crime, found guilty, and sentenced to life in prison. Selena's last album, which was released several months after her death, sold 175,000 copies in one day.

Many other ethnic groups in Texas also have distinctive music that is a part of their history and culture. Cajuns love to sing and

Singer Selena always had a strong Hispanic following, but since her death her popularity has grown and crossed over to white audiences.

Dressed in patriotic fashion, Willie Nelson plays at the Farm Aid IV concert in 1990. The twelve-hour concert to help American farmers featured about seventy singers and groups.

dance to the sounds of an accordion. They often say "Laissez les bons temps roulez," which is French for "Let the good times roll."

ARTISTS AND ART LOVERS

Houstonians John and Dominique de Menil collected thousands of pieces of modern art. When John de Menil died, museums in Paris and New York wanted to buy and display these treasures. Instead of moving the collection, Dominique decided to remain in Houston and build The Menil Collection. The museum, which opened in 1987, rotates displays of more than ten thousand pieces of art. There are also many other fine museums and galleries located throughout the state.

One of the most talented artists in Texas was sculptor Elisabet Ney. She and her husband moved to Texas from Germany during the 1870s. In 1893 Ney was asked to sculpt statues of Sam Houston and Stephen F. Austin for the Texas exhibit at the Chicago World's Fair. Her work created such a sensation that she eventually cut two additional statues from marble to match the originals. The original works are now displayed in the Texas capitol in Austin and the copies can be seen in Statuary Hall in Washington, D.C.

MEDICINE AND TECHNOLOGY

In 1954, Houston surgeon Dr. Michael DeBakey made medical history when he performed heart surgery that was shown on public television. DeBakey became a leader in the field of cardio-

Sculptor Elizabet Ney at work in her studio. Today, the studio is a museum displaying the plaster models of several well-known statues, including Sam Houston and Stephen Austin.

vascular medicine, and in 1964 he performed the nation's first coronary bypass operation. Although he is in his eighties now, Dr. DeBakey still spends long hours in the operating room, performing surgery and training younger doctors. He said: "I try to teach them to strive for excellence in their work. . . . You know, everybody can do better than they think they can if they'd try."

Cardiovascular surgeon Dr. Denton Cooley also did pioneer work in the treatment of heart disease. In 1968, Cooley performed the first successful U.S. heart transplant at the Texas Heart Institute in Houston. A year later, he implanted the world's first artificial heart into a human. Both surgeons practice in the Texas Medical Center, a sprawling complex of hospitals, research laboratories, and medical schools in Houston.

In addition to discoveries in the field of medicine, Texans have also made many important advances in technology. Jack Kilby went to work for Texas Instruments in Dallas in 1958. His job was to find a way to put electronic components together without the use of wires. After a lot of hard work, he developed an integrated circuit made out of silicon. Using the silicon chip, small handheld calculators and personal computers were created that could do the work of much larger machines, and do it faster.

Dallas resident Ross Perot also developed ways to use computers during the 1960s. He started a company called Electronic Data Systems (EDS) that processed information for companies. In 1968, Ross Perot decided to take EDS public and let others buy shares of the company. The price of EDS stock skyrocketed during its first few weeks on the stock exchange. By the end of 1968, Perot was worth $2 billion. Today, Ross Perot is considered to be the richest man in Texas with a net worth of more than $3.5 billion. Perot also became a candidate for president in the 1992 election and amassed a total of nearly twenty million votes.

THE WRITERS

After World War II, J. Frank Dobie and a group of friends met once a month to sit around a campfire and tell stories. Dobie later turned many of those stories into books about the Texas of yesterday. He wrote of longhorns and cowboys, bandits and rattlesnakes. In all, twenty of Dobie's books and hundreds of articles were published.

Writer J. Frank Dobie once wrote of himself, "I'm not a historian in the strictest sense, but I suppose I can be called a historian of the longhorns, the mustangs, the coyote and other characters of the West."

Many of his books are still in print and continue to entertain readers today.

Coronado's Children, published in 1930, contains stories of the desert and buried treasure. In one of the stories, called "The Challenge of the Desert," Dobie tells about a Mexican girl who was herding goats when a windstorm overtook her.

> She had walked less than a hundred yards when she became almost blinded by the driving sand. She lost view of the goats. Then she faced the teeth of the wind to make for the shelter of the little Mexican ranch where she lived. Now the sand was cutting like knives. She tried to bear against it, and veered. She zigzagged. She could not see a foot

away. She let the wind carry her as it would. She never knew how many hours she stumbled, crawled, cried. She lost all sense of time, direction, purpose.

Larry McMurtry writes many books and screenplays that have a Texas setting. *Lonesome Dove*, published in 1985, won a Pulitzer Prize the following year. The story revolves around the adventures of the Hat Creek Outfit as they move a herd of cattle from south

LEON HALE

Since the 1940s, newspaper columnist Leon Hale has been traveling the back roads of Texas, observing people and nature and curiosities. In *Texas Chronicles*, he wrote:

At La Grange I stopped to get gas a couple of blocks west of the courthouse square and I had a few minutes to watch two young boys, walking along the highway toward the Colorado River. Going fishing.

They look about eleven to me, maybe twelve, and this was the first time they'd gone fishing since school turned out for the summer. I could tell by the way they walked, with quick steps and eagerness, wanting to be there now, not ten minutes later but right now.

For a few seconds I was able to feel what those youngsters felt. A sort of anxiety, part pleasant and part uncomfortable. A feeling that says, "Something good is about to happen but I'm not sure I can wait." We used to feel it on the way to going swimming. Or waiting for the soda skeet to draw us big frosty mugs of root beer. Or walking to the picture show on Saturday afternoons.

Texas to Montana. Along the way they meet up with Blue Duck, a renegade Indian who is an expert in the art of torture.

Texas has also been home to other famous writers. Katherine Anne Porter, who was born in Indian Creek, was awarded a Pulitzer Prize in 1966 for a collection of her short stories. And Horton Foote won a Pulitzer Prize in 1995 for his drama, *The Young Man From Atlanta*. He is also an Academy Award winner for his screenplays, *Tender Mercies* and *To Kill a Mockingbird*. Even though Foote lives in New York for much of the year, his heart has never left his boyhood home of Wharton. He said: "When I was a boy, I would rather listen to my grandmother talk than play ball. I was raised in the oral tradition of our heritage. And today, I still hear those stories. They re-create a time, a place, for me."

TEXAS SPORTS MANIA

Sports of all kinds are a popular pastime in Texas. In many small towns, the Friday night high school football game is the highlight of the week. Adults and students alike turn out to cheer the home team to victory. In 1891, the first organized football game in Texas was played in Dallas. After the game, a reporter in the *Dallas Times Herald* wrote: "About the only thing that can be said of the game is that it is the best excuse for falling down that has been invented."

Sports teams have come a long way in Texas since 1891. The state's college teams are among the best in the nation. In professional sports, the Dallas Cowboys were National Football League (NFL) Super Bowl champions in 1993, 1994, and 1996, while the Houston Rockets were National Basketball Association (NBA)

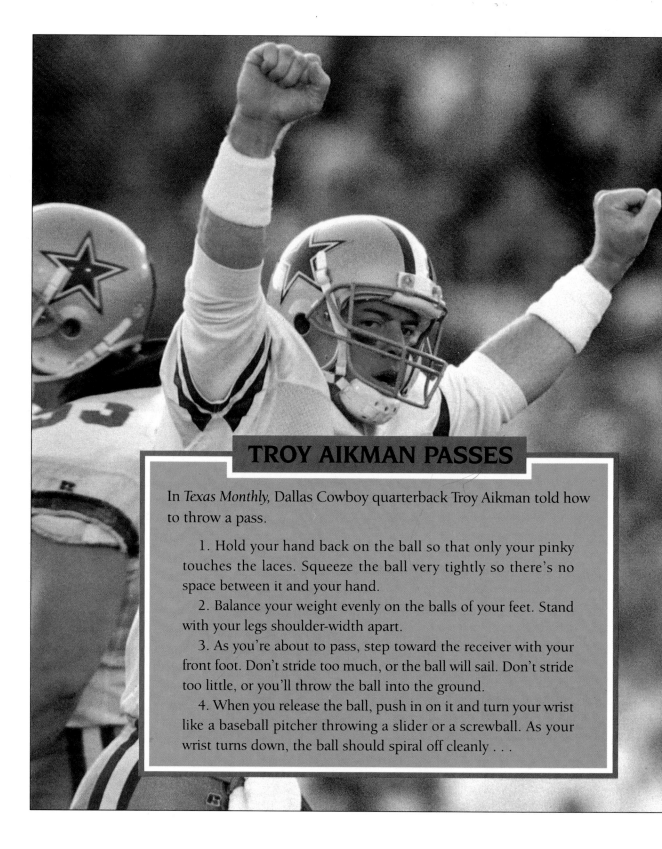

TROY AIKMAN PASSES

In *Texas Monthly,* Dallas Cowboy quarterback Troy Aikman told how to throw a pass.

1. Hold your hand back on the ball so that only your pinky touches the laces. Squeeze the ball very tightly so there's no space between it and your hand.

2. Balance your weight evenly on the balls of your feet. Stand with your legs shoulder-width apart.

3. As you're about to pass, step toward the receiver with your front foot. Don't stride too much, or the ball will sail. Don't stride too little, or you'll throw the ball into the ground.

4. When you release the ball, push in on it and turn your wrist like a baseball pitcher throwing a slider or a screwball. As your wrist turns down, the ball should spiral off cleanly . . .

Houston Rocket Hakeem Olajuwon drives around Los Angeles Clipper Tony Massenburg.

Dallas Cowboy fans celebrate their second consecutive Super Bowl victory in 1994.

champions in 1994 and 1995. Leading the Rockets in scoring is seven-foot center, Hakeem Olajuwon. Growing up in his native country of Nigeria, Olajuwon was often teased about his height. He said: "Sometimes I would be ashamed of being so tall. I would wish

I was normal height so I can be friendly just like everyone else. Everywhere I went, people were looking."

Olajuwon's height turned into an advantage when he started playing basketball at age fifteen. Word of his skill spread, and the tall Nigerian came to the United States to attend school. He first played for the University of Houston before joining the Houston Rockets in 1984. During a Rockets game on November 11, 1995, Olajuwon passed the twenty thousand mark for points scored during his professional career, along with eleven thousand rebounds. Only nine players have reached that total, including basketball greats Wilt Chamberlain and Kareem Abdul-Jabar.

Another record-setting Texas athlete is Nolan Ryan. When he retired from baseball in 1993, the right-handed pitcher held the world record for the most strikeouts with 5,714. In addition, his blazing fastball got past all of the batters in seven games, the most no-hitters on record. All of that pitching can be hard on the hand. As a remedy for calluses, Ryan soaked his right hand in pickle juice.

Texas women have also made a mark on the world of sports. Among the greatest was Mildred Didrikson Zaharias of Port Arthur. As a child playing baseball, she hit so many home runs her friends began to call her "Babe" after Babe Ruth. During high school, she was an all-American in basketball.

When she competed in the 1932 Olympic Games, there were only five events that were open to women, and each competitor could enter only three of them. Babe won a gold medal in the javelin throw, another gold in the 80-meter hurdles, and a silver in the high jump.

In 1935, Babe began to play golf and won every major champi-

The Babe in full swing, 1937

onship between 1940 and 1950. In 1938 she married George Zaharias, a professional wrestler. Babe said that he was attractive to her because "he was the only man she had ever met who could drive a golf ball farther than she could."

Babe Zaharias was diagnosed with cancer in 1950, the year after the Associated Press named her the outstanding woman athlete of the century. Six years later she died, with her golf clubs beside her in the hospital room.

In addition to its share of talented and well-known people, Texas is also full of spectacular places. Travelers do not have to look far to find beautiful scenery and interesting historical areas to visit.

6 TRAVEL THROUGH TEXAS

A tour of Texas logically begins in Austin, which has been the state capital since 1845. Named for Stephen F. Austin, the city is located on the banks of the Colorado River in a scenic, hilly part of Texas. Central to Austin is the state capitol building, which was completed in 1888. A special railroad line was built at the time of construction to haul the rose granite from a nearby quarry.

By 1988, the 100-year-old building was in need of major repair work. Also, the state government had grown and the legislators needed more office space. A massive, $200 million project was started in 1989 that restored the fine old structure to its former beauty. In addition, a huge underground extension was built behind the original building.

Other Austin attractions include the University of Texas campus and the Congress Avenue Bridge. More than half a million Mexican free-tailed bats make their home under the bridge from March until November every year. In the evenings, people gather in the area to watch as clouds of bats fly into the night sky in search of insects to eat.

About eighty miles southwest of Austin is San Antonio, where Spain built five missions in the 1700s. The most famous of these is the Alamo. Today the site has been restored, and visitors can walk through the chapel and long barracks, where Texans fought

At the Congress Avenue Bridge in Houston, watching Mexican free-tailed bats is a favorite form of evening entertainment.

for their independence from Mexico. Exhibits include Davy Crockett's rifle, Old Betsy, and the ring William Travis placed on a string around the neck of little Angelina Dickenson before he died.

The meandering San Antonio River winds through the city near the Alamo grounds. There are many restaurants and interesting shops along The River Walk, which is paved with cobblestones and surrounded by beautiful trees and shrubs. Sight-seeing barges are also available for those who want to tour the historic area by boat. During the annual Fiesta, it is traditional for revelers to race up and down the Riverwalk, bashing each other with *cascarones*, which are eggshells filled with confetti.

The Alamo decorated for Christmas. This symbol of Texan independence is the most visited site in Texas.

San Antonio's large Latino population has influenced the city's culture a great deal. Souvenirs can be found at El Mercado, a marketplace crammed with stalls full of Mexican crafts and food. Also, in keeping with its Mexican history, the outside of the new San Antonio Public Library was painted with a color called "enchilada red."

Mexican influence continues to grow as we move further south toward the Rio Grande. Laredo, which is located on the border between Texas and Mexico, is as much Mexican as it is American. Both Spanish and English are spoken in all of the stores, and goods are often paid for with Mexican pesos instead of dollars. Just across the Rio Grande from Laredo is the Mexican town of Nuevo Laredo. Residents of both towns cross back and forth across the border to work and shop.

Farther west, at the spot where the Rio Grande meets the sea, is the beginning of a long barrier island. In 1962, the northern eighty miles of the island became the Padre Island National Seashore. Its

The Fiesta San Antonio

Guacomole is a favorite "Tex-Mex" dish that is made of mashed-up avocados and spices.

An aerial view of the beaches of Padre Island National Seashore

protected beaches are home to hundreds of bird and plant species. Visitors to the area often camp and fish along the empty, unbroken miles of shoreline. Jutting out into the surf are hundreds of fishing piers, where anglers drop their lines into the water, day or night, to see what bites. Veteran shark fisherman Happy Sites said: "It doesn't matter if I catch one or somebody else does. I just love to be out here."

Just inland from the National Seashore is Corpus Christi, sometimes called "the Sparkling City by the Sea." Tourists walk along the

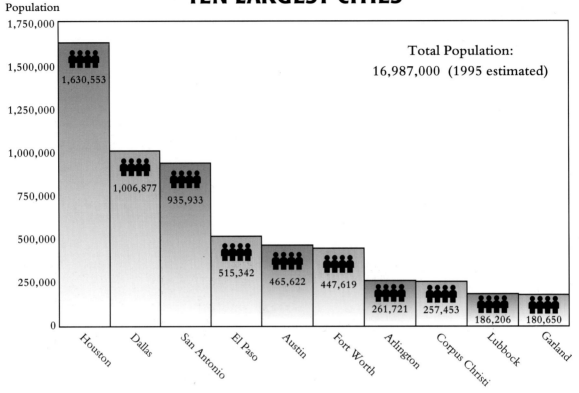

TEN LARGEST CITIES

Population

Total Population:
16,987,000 (1995 estimated)

Houston	1,630,553
Dallas	1,006,877
San Antonio	935,933
El Paso	515,342
Austin	465,622
Fort Worth	447,619
Arlington	261,721
Corpus Christi	257,453
Lubbock	186,206
Garland	180,650

two-mile seawall of Shoreline Drive, watching sailboats skim across the water of Corpus Christi Bay. Children throw bread crumbs to the clouds of hungry seagulls that squawk in the balmy air. Also facing the bay is the Texas State Aquarium, where visitors can watch sharks, rays, and tropical fish swim in huge saltwater tanks.

About two hundred miles north of Corpus Christi is Houston, the largest city in Texas. Located in Houston is the San Jacinto Monument, which marks the site where Texas won its independence from Mexico on April 21, 1836. Elevators inside the monument take visitors to the top of the 570-foot structure for a look at the Houston ship channel and city skyline. The San Jacinto Museum features exhibits that follow Texas history from its earliest days to the present.

South of the historic battlefield is the Lyndon B. Johnson Space Center, where astronauts are trained for missions in space. Visitors to the center get to touch a moon rock, walk through a space station training module, and peek inside the small capsules that carried America's first astronauts into space during the 1960s. When astronauts first landed on the moon on July 20, 1969, Neil

SAN JACINTO DAY

In 1890, survivors of the Battle of San Jacinto gathered at the site to mark the location of the Texan and Mexican camps. The San Jacinto battleground was later purchased by the state of Texas and developed into a 1,000-acre historical park. Central to the park is a 570-foot monument that was built to commemorate the spot where Texas won independence from Mexico on April 21, 1836.

Every year, the victory is remembered with a living history celebration. One hundred fifty participants, dressed in leather britches and fringed boots, set up Texan and Mexican camps that reflect conditions in 1836. As the men sit around blazing fires, they polish nineteenth-century muskets, swords, and bayonets. At four-thirty in the afternoon, the Texans fire a cannon and advance on the Mexican camp to reenact the twenty-minute battle. To conclude the ceremonies, a tribute is read in English and Spanish and a wreath is laid to honor all who died at the Battle of San Jacinto.

Armstrong said: "Houston, Tranquility Base here. The Eagle has landed."

East of Houston, the Texas coast gently curves to meet the Louisiana border. Along that border is the most heavily wooded area in the state. The smell of pine trees fills the air in the Piney Woods region within the Big Thicket National Preserve. Fishermen visit the area to cast their lines into the many rivers and streams that flow among the trees. Campsites are available to people who want to escape the noise and smog of the cities in the cool, quiet woods.

When it is time for the campers to pack up and leave, many return to their homes in cities such as Dallas and Fort Worth. Dallas will always be remembered as the place where President John Kennedy was assassinated on November 22, 1963. The site of that tragedy, which was named a National Historic Landmark in 1993, is a grim reminder of the violence that plagues America.

Dallas, which started as just one log cabin in 1841, is today a city of skyscrapers, museums, fine hotels, and big business. Just next to Dallas and half its size is Fort Worth, which is sometimes called "Cowtown." Fort Worth got its start during the days of the long trail drives, when its stockyards were the biggest in the world. Today there are restaurants and shops in an area where thousands of cattle were once penned. In June, the Chisholm Trail Roundup is held in the Fort Worth Stockyards. The celebration begins with a trail drive and also features a chili cook-off, parade, and rodeo.

Moving northwest from Fort Worth, travelers cross the Palo Duro Canyon on their way to the north of Texas. It was in this canyon that Comanches made their last stand, before surrendering in 1875

PLACES TO SEE

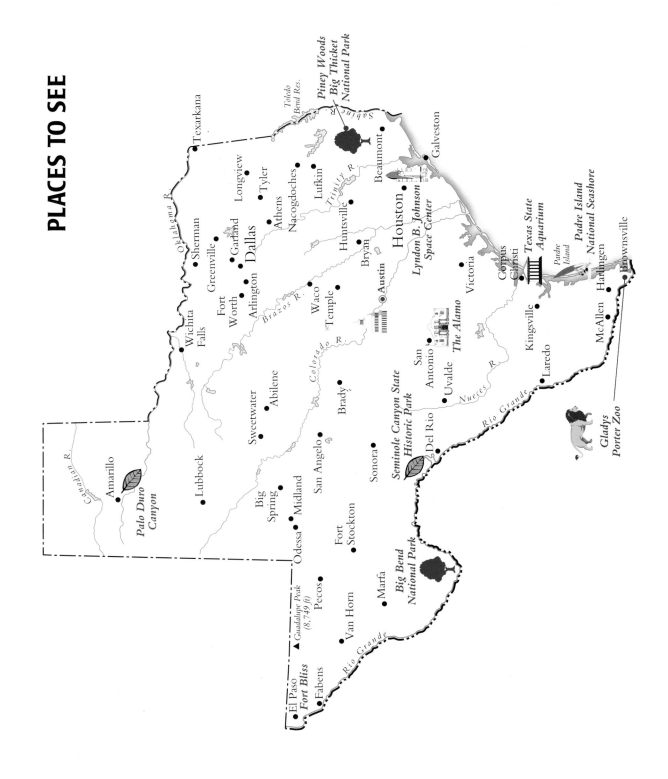

Texarkana

Oklahoma R.

*Toledo
Bend Res.*

Piney Woods
Big Thicket
National Park

Sabine R.

Longview
Sherman
Tyler
Athens
Nacogdoches
Lufkin
Greenville
Garland
Dallas
Arlington
Fort
Worth
Huntsville
Bryan

Trinity R.

Beaumont
Galveston

Houston

Lyndon B. Johnson
Space Center

Wichita
Falls

Austin

Texas State
Aquarium

Corpus
Christi

Padre Island
National Seashore

Brazos R.

Waco
Temple

Victoria

Padre
Island

Sweetwater
Abilene

The Alamo

San
Antonio

Kingsville

Hardlingen
McAllen
Brownsville

Colorado R.

Brady

Uvalde

Laredo

Nueces R.

Lubbock

San Angelo

Sonora

Seminole Canyon State
Historic Park

Del Rio

Rio Grande

Gladys
Porter Zoo

Canadian R.

Amarillo

Palo Duro
Canyon

Big
Spring
Midland
Odessa

Fort
Stockton

Marfa

Big Bend
National Park

Pecos

▲ *Guadalupe Peak*
(8,749 ft)

Van Horn

Rio Grande

El Paso
Fort Bliss
Fabens

to U.S. troops. Visitors to the area can take a ride along the canyon bottom on the Sad Monkey Railroad. The more adventurous ones rent horses and ride over the rugged landscape.

Twenty miles north of Palo Duro Canyon is the town of Amarillo, complete with modern buildings, oil, and cattle. The largest livestock auctions in the state are held in the Amarillo stockyards, where more than six hundred thousand head of cattle are bought and sold every year. While spending time in Amarillo, visitors sometimes tour the Alibates Flint Quarries National Monument. It was here that Native Americans gathered flint for their arrowheads, spear points, and tools more than twelve thousand years ago. Park ranger Ed Day said: "The Indians could make almost any kind of tool or weapon with this rock. Flint is so hard that you can scratch your pocketknife with it."

South of Amarillo are Midland and Odessa. Both are oil towns that grew after 1923, when huge quantities of petroleum were discovered in the Permian Basin. Midland is home to the Confederate Air Force, an organization that restores and flies World War II aircraft. More than one hundred planes are on display in a museum that also features military uniforms and war memorabilia.

When sightseers leave Midland and Odessa to travel west, there is little to greet them on the way to El Paso except small towns, big ranches, and a vast blue sky. This is the driest part of Texas—cowboy country.

Nestled in a bowl of mountains, El Paso was home to Spanish missionaries as far back as 1680. The Tiguas, who were refugees from a Pueblo Indian revolt in New Mexico, came to El Paso in 1681. They helped build the Ysleta Mission, which has been restored and is located on the Tigua Indian Reservation. Visitors to the reservation watch demonstrations of pottery making, weaving, and tribal dances.

Also located in El Paso is Fort Bliss, which was established in 1849 to help protect the United States border with Mexico. There are several museums on the historic site that trace the history of the fort from frontier times. Today, twenty thousand American troops are stationed at Fort Bliss, the largest air-defense base in the United States.

As the Rio Grande flows south from El Paso, it slices through the mountain ranges of Big Bend National Park. Comanches and Apaches once hunted in the wild and rugged terrain. More than one hundred years ago, an unidentified Mexican vaquero (cowboy) said that it was an area "where the rainbows wait for the rain, and the big river is kept in a stone box, and water runs uphill and mountains float in the air."

In the park, there are several hundred miles of trails. Visitors are able to hike to some areas, but need horses to get to others. Several visitor centers that are scattered around the area offer food and maps along with advice from park rangers. Campsites are also available for tourists who want to stay in the park overnight.

As the Rio Grande continues on its southward path through Big Bend, it flows near the Seminole Canyon State Historical Park. In some of the rock shelters that surround the canyon, ancient Native American paintings are still visible on the stone walls. The many colorful pictographs, which are some of the oldest in the country, were painted more than four thousand years ago. The prehistoric artists made paint out of minerals that they had dug from the soil

A mist settles around the Chisnos Mountains, whose name means "ghosts" in Spanish.

and then mixed with animal fat. Using their fingers, along with brushes made from plants, the early people painted animals, human figures, and weapons on the rocky surfaces.

The last stop on the path of the Rio Grande in Texas is Brownsville, located near the southern tip of the state. Palm trees and bougainvillea grow in the tropical air of the port city. In the Gladys Porter Zoo, which has been named one of the ten best zoos in the country, nearly two thousand birds, mammals, and reptiles are on display in natural settings that have no bars. Just across the border from Brownsville is the Mexican city of Matamoros. The two bridges that connect the cities are filled with tourists much of the time. In Matamoros, shoppers find plenty to buy, including jewelry, pottery, and wood carvings.

Our journey around Texas ends where it began, at the mouth of the Rio Grande. It is winter and the swimmers and sun bathers are gone. A few hardy beach combers wade through the cold water, searching for sand dollars and sea shells. Whitecaps dot the swells offshore as colder air invades the state. Before long, though, the cold will once again give way to warmer days. Bluebonnets and Indian paintbrush will fill the fields and roadsides as they announce the arrival of spring. And people will pack their cars and head for the nearest park, beach, or lake to enjoy a holiday in the warm Texas sun.

THE FLAG: *Called the Lone Star Flag, it has three parts: a white horizontal stripe, a red horizontal stripe, and a blue vertical stripe with a white five-pointed star in its center. The red stands for bravery, the white for purity and the blue for loyalty. Between 1836 and 1845, Texas was a separate country called the Republic of Texas, and this was its official flag. It was adopted by the Third Congress of the Republic on January 25, 1839. When Texas joined the United States in 1845, the Lone Star Flag became the state flag. It is from this flag that Texas got its nickname.*

THE SEAL: *The seal was first adopted on December 10, 1836, as the Great Seal of the Republic of Texas. When Texas became a state, it was changed slightly and adopted as the official state seal, which is still in use today.*

STATE SURVEY

Statehood: December 29, 1845

Origin of Name: The word Texas, or *Tejas* in Spanish, comes from a Caddo word meaning "friends" or "allies."

Nickname: The Lone Star State

Capital: Austin

Motto: Friendship

Bird: Mockingbird

Fish: Guadalupe bass

Flower: Bluebonnet

Tree: Pecan

Gem: Texas blue topaz

Folk Dance: The square dance

Fruit: Texas red grapefruit

Dish: Chili

Mockingbird

Field of bluebonnets

TEXAS, OUR TEXAS

"Texas, Our Texas" was adopted by the Texas legislature as the official state song in May 1929.

Words by Gladys Y. Marsh and William J. Marsh
Music by William J. Marsh

Tex - as, our Tex - as! all hail the might - y State!

Tex - as, our Tex - as! So won - der - ful and great!

Bold - est and grand - est, with - stand - ing ev - 'ry test; O,

Em - pire wide and glo - rious, You stand su - preme - ly blest.

God bless you, Tex - as! And keep you brave and strong, That

you may grow in power and worth, Thro' - out the a - ges long.

GEOGRAPHY

Highest Point: Guadalupe Peak in far West Texas—8,749 feet

Lowest Point: The Gulf of Mexico, at sea level

Area: 267,300 square miles, 7 percent of the area of the United States

Greatest Distance North to South: 800 miles

Greatest Distance East to West: 770 miles

Borders: Oklahoma to the north; Arkansas, Louisiana, and the Gulf of Mexico to the east; New Mexico to the west; Mexico to the south

Hottest Recorded Temperature: 120°F at Seymour on August 12, 1936

Coldest Recorded Temperature: 23°F at Tulia on February 12, 1899, and at Seminole on February 8, 1933

Average Annual Precipitation: 27.21 inches

Major Rivers: Rio Grande, Red, Sabine, Colorado, Brazos, Trinity, Canadian, Pecos, San Antonio, Guadalupe, Neches, Nueces

Major Lakes: Caddo Lake in Northeast Texas is the only major natural lake.

Trees: black gum, cypress, elm, hickory, huisache, magnolia, mesquite, oak, pecan, pine, post oak, sweet gum, Texas mountain laurel, tupelo, walnut

Wild Plants: bluebonnet, buffalo grass, Indiangrass, Indian paintbrush, Mexican hat, prickly pear, ragweed, sideoats grama, tumblegrass, yucca

Animals: alligator, nine-banded armadillo, badger, bat, beaver, bighorn sheep, bison, black bear, black-tailed jack rabbit, bobcat, cougar (mountain lion), coyote, gopher, gray fox, horned lizard, jaguarundi, javelina, kit fox, mink, mole, mule deer, muskrat, ocelot, opossum, raccoon, skunk, snake, white-tailed deer, yellow-haired porcupine

Birds: great horned owl, quail, mottled duck, sandhill crane, turkey, wood stork

Fish: catfish, largemouth bass, sunfish

Endangered Plants: black lace cactus, Texas wild rice, Navasota ladies' tresses orchid, Texas snowbells, Texas trailing phlox, Texas poppy mallow, large-fruited sand verbena

Endangered Animals: black bear, black-footed ferret, coati, finback whale, gray wolf, jaguar, manatee, Mexican long-nosed bat, Mexican wolf, ocelot, red wolf, sperm whale, aplomado falcon, bald eagle, brown pelican, black-capped vireo, peregrine falcon, red-cockaded woodpecker, whooping crane, Chihuahuan mud turtle, concho water snake, hawksbill turtle, Kemp's ridley sea turtle, leatherback turtle, logger-head turtle, northern cat-eyed snake, smooth green snake, speckled racer, Big Bend gambusia, blackfin goby, blunt-nose shiner, fountain darter, paddlefish, shovelnose sturgeon

Red Wolf

TIMELINE

Texas History

1528 Spanish explorer Álvar Núñez Cabeza de Vaca and Moroccan slave Estéban are shipwrecked on the Gulf Coast

1541 Francisco Vásquez de Coronado discovers Palo Duro Canyon

1681 Spanish Franciscan missionaries establish Ysleta, oldest European settlement in Texas

1685 René-Robert Cavelier, Sieur de la Salle builds Fort St. Louis

1700s Comanches move into Texas

1718 Spanish Franciscan missionaries establish the Alamo mission

1758 Comanches destroy San Saba Mission

1821 Texas becomes part of Mexico; first settlers arrive at Stephen F. Austin's land grant

1835 Texans challenge Mexicans at Gonzales

1836 Texans declare independence from Mexico; Mexicans defeat Texans at the Alamo; Texans win victory at San Jacinto; the Republic of Texas is declared

1839 Cherokees are defeated and driven out of the Republic of Texas

1845 Texas joins the United States

1846 Mexican War begins in Texas

1848 Treaty of Guadalupe Hidalgo

1850 Compromise of 1850 creates present-day Texas boundaries

1853 The first Texas railroad begins operation

1861 Texas joins the Confederacy in the Civil War

1865 Slaves in Texas are emancipated

1875 Comanches led by Quanah Parker are defeated by U.S. Cavalry troops

1900 Galveston hurricane kills 6,000 people

1901 Anthony Lucas discovers oil at Spindletop

1919 Texas approves women's right to vote

1925 Miriam "Ma" Ferguson becomes the first woman elected governor of Texas

1932 Texan "Babe" Didrickson wins two gold medals and one silver medal at the Olympics

1941–1945 During World War II, 750,000 Texans serve in the military

1950 Herman Marion Sweatt becomes the first African American admitted to the University of Texas Law School

1958 Jack Kilby invents the integrated circuit at Texas Instruments

1961 The National Aeronautics and Space Administration (NASA) opens the Manned Spacecraft Center in Houston

1963 President John F. Kennedy is assassinated in Dallas

1965 The Astrodome, the world's first air-conditioned football and baseball stadium, opens in Houston

1986 Texas celebrates its sesquicentennial (150 years) of independence

1990 Ann Richards is the second woman to be elected governor

1993 A 51-day standoff between federal law-enforcement officers and Branch Davidians ends in fiery disaster at the cult's compound in Waco

ECONOMY

Manufactured Products: petroleum products, chemicals, aeronautic equipment, electronics, computers, paper, furniture, glass, rubber, lumber, textiles, clothing

Agricultural Products: wheat, cotton, corn, grain sorghum, rice, soybeans, sugar cane, hay, rye, maize, aloe vera, cottonseed products, citrus fruits, vegetables, dairy products, sugar beets, cattle, sheep, fish and seafood, beef products, wool, mohair, hogs, goats, chickens, horses

Crab fisherman

Natural Resources: Lumber, oil, natural gas, coal, iron, native asphalt, granite, marble, sulphur, copper, lead, zinc, helium

Business and Trade: wholesale and retail trade, tourism, banking, insurance, communications, health care and health research, computer industry, state government, electronics, shipping, rail transport, aerospace, farming, ranching

CALENDAR OF CELEBRATIONS

Martin Luther King, Jr.'s birthday, observed on the third Monday in January, honors the African-American minister, non-violent civil rights leader, and Nobel Peace Prize winner. State employees, federal employees, and students enjoy a holiday from work and school.

Texas Independence Day, March 2, is a state holiday celebrated throughout Texas with picnics, barbecues, parades, and fireworks after sundown.

San Jacinto Day, April 21, is a state holiday celebrating the Texas army's victory at the Battle of San Jacinto, led by General Sam Houston. This battle established Texas' independence from Mexico. Many Texans visit the San Jacinto Battleground and San Jacinto Monument near Houston on this holiday.

Cinco de Mayo, May 5, is celebrated in many cities throughout Texas and Mexico. It marks Mexico's final rejection of European rule in 1867. In Austin's Fiesta Gardens, flamenco dancers and Tejano musicians highlight the day's festivities. In Uvalde, the day's ceremonies include raising the U.S. flag at Jardin de los Heros Park.

Juneteenth or **Emancipation Day**, a state holiday commemorating the freeing of slaves, is celebrated on June 19. Texans of African descent traditionally take a holiday from work to celebrate this day with family reunions and picnic feasts. It was not a legal holiday, however, until 1980.

A turn-of-the-century Juneteenth celebration

Lyndon B. Johnson's birthday, August 27, is a state holiday honoring this native Texan, the thirty-sixth president of the United States. Texans can make the scenic drive to Johnson City in Central Texas and visit Johnson's boyhood home, then picnic in a nearby state park.

Fiestas Patrias, September 16, is Mexican Independence Day, celebrating the anniversary of the first move to end European dominance in

Mexico. The celebration begins on September 15 each year, when Mexican Texans have large parties, dress in traditional clothing, eat special foods, and dance and sing to Mexican music.

The State Fair of Texas is held every year during September and October in Dallas at the huge Fair Park fairgrounds, whose stadium is also the site of the annual Cotton Bowl. Thousands of Texans and visitors attend the festivities and take part in the amusements and enjoy refreshments like hot buttered corn-on-the-cob.

Octoberfest is celebrated in early October, especially in the central Texas German communities of New Braunfels and Fredericksburg. Octoberfests began in the mid-1800s with large gatherings of German-American singing societies called Saengerfests and Volkfests. Today, Texans of all backgrounds gather for several days to celebrate German culture, especially German music, dancing, and food.

Dia de los Muertos (Day of the Dead), November 1 and 2, is the Mexican version of the Roman Catholic All Saints Day or All Souls Day. It is a special Mexican mix of pre-Columbian homage to ancestors and Catholic ritual. In Austin, the holiday is marked with a special parade down Congress Avenue. It includes skeleton-decorated floats, ceremonial altars, and "low-rider" vehicles.

STATE STARS

Alvin Ailey

Alvin Ailey (1931–1989), African-American dancer and choreographer, was born in Rogers but moved to Los Angeles at age 12. He began formal dance training in high school and after college founded the Alvin Ailey American Dance Theatre in New York. In 1965, his company made a successful tour of Europe, receiving an amazing 61 curtain calls in Hamburg, Germany.

Stephen F. Austin (1793–1836) obtained a land grant from Mexico in 1821 and founded a colony in Texas of 300 Anglo-Americans. As settlements grew, he tried to keep peace between the Mexican government and the Anglo settlers. But after he was wrongly imprisoned in Mexico, he helped the Texas Revolution and was elected the first secretary of state of the new Texas Republic. The city of Austin was named in his honor.

Gail Borden (1801–1874), a New Yorker, settled in Texas in 1829. He worked on several unsuccessful inventions but went bankrupt and returned to the Northeast. In 1856 he received a patent for condensing milk in a vacuum and opened a plant. When the Civil War broke out, Borden's canned milk, which wouldn't spoil, was in demand by the Union Army. Later the general public also began buying it, and Borden returned to Texas. A town and a county there are named for him.

Carol Burnett (1933–   ), television comedian and film actor, was born in San Antonio. She first gained national attention on TV's *Garry Moore Show* in 1956. For an amazing 11 years (1967–1978), she hosted her own comedy TV program, *The Carol Burnett Show,* and became a household name. Her film credits include *A Wedding, The Four Seasons, Annie,* and the Emmy-award winning *Friendly Fire.*

Earl Campbell (1955–   ), born in Tyler, gained fame as a running back with the University of Texas Longhorns. In his four years at UT he rushed for 4,444 yards and was named to the All-Conference team four times. The Texas legislature officially designated him a "state legend," and he won the Heisman Memorial Trophy in 1977. He was elected to the Pro Football Hall of Fame in 1991.

Earl Campbell

Henry G. Cisneros

Henry G. Cisneros (1947–   ), statesman born in San Antonio, gained prominence as the first Hispanic mayor of a major U.S. city when he was elected in San Antonio in 1981. In 1993 he was appointed Secretary of Housing and Urban Development (HUD) by President Bill Clinton.

Van Cliburn (1934–   ), pianist from Kilgore, won a statewide piano competition at age 12. At 13, he made his debut with the Houston Symphony, and the next year he played at Carnegie Hall in New York. In 1958 he became the first American to win the gold medal at the International Tchaikovsky Competition in Russia. He returned to a tickertape parade in New York and a reception at the White House from President Dwight Eisenhower.

Horton Foote (1916–   ), playwright and screenwriter, was born in Wharton. He received his first Academy Award in 1962 for writing the screenplay of *To Kill a Mockingbird*. He won his second Oscar in 1983 for his screenplay of *Tender Mercies*. He also wrote screenplays for *The Trip to Bountiful, 1918,* and *On Valentine's Day,* all set in Texas. In 1995 he won the Pulitzer Prize for his play *The Young Man from Atlanta.*

John Nance Garner (1868–1967) of Uvalde was elected to the U.S. House of Representatives in 1902. He served there for 30 years. Known as "Cactus Jack," he became speaker of the House in 1931 and U.S. vice president in 1932, when Franklin D. Roosevelt became president. During his two terms as "VP," Garner pushed New Deal legislation through Congress. But he would not support FDR's bid for a third term as president, and he lost the nomination himself.

Henry B. Gonzalez (1916–   ) was born in San Antonio. In 1956 he became the first Mexican American elected to the state Senate since 1846. In 1961 he became the first Mexican American elected from Texas to the U.S. House of Representatives. At age 78 in 1994, while serving his thirty-third year in Congress, Gonzalez accepted the Profile of Courage award, the only Texan ever to win it.

Oveta Culp Hobby (1916–1995) of Houston became the first director of the Women's Army Corps (WACs) in 1942. She was the first woman to attain the rank of colonel and to receive the Army's Distinguished Service Medal. In the 1950s she was the first secretary of the Department of Health, Education, and Welfare. In 1964, after the death of her husband, she took his job as publisher of *The Houston Post*. She was the first woman elected director of the American Society of Newspaper Editors.

Ben Hogan (1912–   ) of Fort Worth started his golfing career as a caddie at age 11. He electrified the golf world in 1946 when he won several major tournaments and took first place among money winners. He remained on top for 10 years, winning the U.S. Open four times, even after an auto accident almost killed him in 1949. In 1950, a commission of sports writers named him one of the greatest golfers of the twentieth century.

Buddy Holly (1936–1959), born in Lubbock, was a songwriter and pioneer of rock-and-roll music. He had a strong and widespread influence on musicians such as the Beatles and Eric Clapton. Holly and his band, the Crickets, were among the first white rock bands to play their own songs. Holly wrote most of their hits, including "That'll Be the Day," "Peggy Sue," "Rave On," and "Maybe Baby." He died in a plane crash at age 23.

Sam Houston (1793–1863) was sent to Texas in 1832 by President Andrew Jackson to negotiate with Indians. Houston was soon caught up in the fight for Texas independence. As the commander of the small outnumbered Texas army, he won the Battle San Jacinto. He was the Texas Republic's first president and a U.S. senator for nearly 14 years. Elected governor in 1859, he opposed Texas secession from the Union. When the Civil War broke out, he retired to Huntsville, where his home is now preserved as a museum.

John Arthur "Jack" Johnson (1878–1946) was a prizefighter born in Galveston. He was boxing's first African-American heavyweight champion of the world. He won the title in 1908 in Sydney, Australia, and remained world champion for seven years. His career included 80 wins, 7 losses, and 14 draws. He died following an automobile accident in North Carolina.

Lady Bird Johnson (1912–   ), born in Karnack, was First Lady to President Lyndon B. Johnson and the force behind the Highway Beautification Act passed by Congress in 1965. She founded the National Wildflower Research Center near Austin in 1982. In 1993, she presided over the ground-breaking ceremony for the center's new 42-acre site. It is the only nonprofit environmental organization dedicated to the study, preservation, and replanting of native plants.

Lyndon Baines Johnson (1908–1973), born near Stonewall, became an influential member of the U.S. House of Representatives and the Senate. As vice president he became president after the assassination of President John F. Kennedy in 1963. During his presidency, "LBJ" used his power gained from years in Congress to pass many civil rights programs. They include the Civil Rights Act of 1964 and the Voting Rights Act of 1965. Reelected by a landslide, he lost popularity during his second term because of the Vietnam War.

Tommy Lee Jones (1946–   ), an actor born in San Saba, attended Harvard University on scholarship. He got his acting start in the early 1970s in *One Life to Live*, a TV "soap." In 1976, film work took him to Hollywood, where he earned enough to buy a ranch in Texas. He won an Emmy Award for *The Executioner's Song* and an Oscar for *The Fugitive*. Other film credits include *JFK, The Client, Blue Sky*, and *Blown Away*.

Scott Joplin (1868–1917), born in Texarkana, was the son of a freed slave. He is credited with inventing ragtime music. He composed more than 500 music pieces, including a ballet and two operas. But his best-known tunes are "rags," or ragtime songs. His rag "The Entertainer" revived ragtime in 1973, when it was the theme of the Oscar-winning film *The Sting*. Although Joplin died in poverty, never to know fame during his lifetime, he was awarded a Pulitzer Prize in 1976 for his contributions to American music.

Barbara Jordan (1936–1996), born in Houston, was awarded the Medal of Freedom, the nation's highest civilian honor, in 1994. She began her political career in 1966, when she became the first black woman elected to the Texas Senate. In 1972, she was elected as a U.S. representative, and she won national recognition serving on the Judiciary Committee during the investigation of the Watergate scandal. In her final years, she was a professor at the Lyndon B. Johnson School of Public Affairs at The University of Texas, Austin.

Audie Murphy (1924–1971), born in Farmersville, was the most decorated soldier in World War II. He won the Medal of Honor, the Distinguished Service Cross, and the Purple Heart. When he returned from the war in 1945, not yet 21 years old, he was greeted by parades all over Texas. Murphy wrote a best-selling book about his war experiences titled *To Hell and Back* and starred in several Hollywood films in the 1940s and 1950s. He died in an airplane crash.

Larry McMurtry (1936–   ), author born in Wichita Falls, has written many best-selling novels. Among them are *Horseman Pass By*, *The Last Picture Show*, *Terms of Endearment*, and *Texasville*—all made into films. His Western novel *Lonesome Dove* won the 1986 Pulitzer Prize for fiction and was also made into a television film.

Willie Nelson (1933–   ), born in Abbott, began his songwriting career in Nashville. His hit songs earned him a spot in the Nashville Songwriters Hall of Fame. Since returning to Texas in 1972, he has contributed to the growth and popularity of Texas music through his personal appearances, hit albums, and gold records such as "Blue Eyes Cryin' in the Rain." Nelson has sponsored music festivals to benefit farmers, hosted many famous Fourth of July picnics, and starred in films.

Quanah Parker (1847–1911), Comanche chief, was the son of Chief Peta Nocona and captive white woman Cynthia Ann Parker, who lived with the Comanches for 24 years. Quanah became the last great Comanche war chief at age 19, leading his people first in a war against the Anglos, then during peacetime after surrendering in 1875. He went to Washington, D.C., for the inauguration of President Theodore Roosevelt and negotiated with the U.S. government on behalf of Indians.

H. Ross Perot (1930–   ), born in Texarkana, was named the richest person in Texas in 1993. His net worth then was estimated at $3.5 billion. He amassed his fortune in the computer industry, founding Electronic Data Systems (EDS) in 1962, which he later sold. In 1988 he founded Perot Systems, which now competes with EDS. Perot gained national attention during his unsuccessful $60-million campaign for president in 1992.

Katherine Anne Porter (1890–1980), short story writer and novelist, was born in Indian Creek. She was best known for her brilliant short stories until 1962, when her novel *Ship of Fools* appeared. It was made into a feature film with an all-star cast. She won the Pulitzer Prize in 1966 for

The Collected Stories. She also wrote *Flowering Judas, Pale Horse, Pale Rider,* and *The Leaning Tower.*

Robert Rauschenburg (1925–   ), an artist born in Port Arthur, became a painter after serving in the navy during World War II. He studied art at the Art Students League in New York City and had his first one-man show there in 1951. Before age 30 he shocked the art world with his "combines," sculptural works made from found objects and paint. (One was a stuffed goat with a rubber tire around its middle.) From 1960 on he mainly made paintings and collages, becoming a world-renowned force in modern art.

Sam Rayburn (1882–1961), known as "Mr. Sam," grew up on a farm and practiced law in Bonham. In 1912 he was elected to the U.S. House of Representatives. He was reelected 24 times and served for almost 49 years, a record. In the 1930s he helped create New Deal legislation. He became speaker of the House in 1940 and held the post for 17 years, also a record. A staunch Democrat, Rayburn won support for his policies from members of both parties, and he was one of the most powerful speakers in U. S. history.

Ann Richards (1933–   ), born in Lakeview, became in 1982 the first woman to be elected state treasurer. In 1988 she captured the public eye by delivering the keynote address at the Democratic convention and saying that Republican candidate George H. W. Bush was "born with a silver foot in his mouth." Elected governor of Texas in 1990, the second woman to hold that office, she appointed many Hispanics, blacks, and women to state offices. She lost her 1994 bid for reelection to George W. Bush, son of the former president.

Nolan Ryan

Nolan Ryan (1947–   ), baseball pitcher, was born in Refugio. On May 1, 1991, he pitched his seventh career no-hitter—setting a record in baseball history—while playing for the Texas Rangers against the Toronto Blue Jays. The native Texan also holds the world's record for the most strike-outs (5,714) and the most walks: 2,795 between 1968 and 1993.

Lee Trevino (1939–   ), born in Dallas, was a good golfer by age 17. After service in the marines, he played in his first Professional Golfers' Association (PGA) meet in 1966. In 1967 he was named Rookie of the Year. In 1968 he won the U.S. Open championship, setting a record as the first player to win with four below-par rounds. After a slump early in 1971, he came back later that year to be the first player ever to win the U.S., Canadian, and British Opens in one year.

Tommy Tune (1939–   ), choreographer and director, was born in Houston. Unusually tall for a dancer, he was a standout in Broadway musicals such as *Bye Bye Birdie* and *My One and Only*. He soon went from dancing to choreography and directed *Nine, Grand Hotel,* and *The Will Rogers Follies*, all major hits. By 1994 when he had won nine Tony awards, Tune was the most successful choreographer-director of American musicals.

Victorio (18??–1880), Mimbreno Apache chief, was the last Native American leader in the nineteenth century to wage war against Texas. In 1878, a special regiment of U.S. Cavalry was sent to the Trans-Pecos region of West Texas to stop Victorio's raids on white settlements, both there and in Mexico. He escaped capture for two years, but in 1880, the Mexican Army, which had joined the chase, found and killed him.

Mildred "Babe" Didrikson Zaharias (1914–1956), an athlete, grew up in Beaumont. She got the nickname "Babe" (after Babe Ruth) while hitting home runs in sandlot baseball, and she also played basketball. In a national track meet in 1932, she won the team championship—all by herself. At the Olympic Games in Los Angeles that year, she won three medals and set two world records. As a professional golfer she won every major golf title between 1940 and 1950. Before dying from cancer, Babe played benefits for cancer research.

TOUR THE STATE

Amon Carter Museum of Western Art, Fort Worth, displays one of the nation's best collections of Western art and photography. Nearby is the **Kimball Art Museum**, which shows modern American and European art in an unusual and award-winning building.

Sundance Square, Fort Worth, boasts a luxury hotel, restaurants, and shops in restored old buildings downtown. The site is named for the Sundance Kid, who in 1898 lived in this neighborhood with his sidekick Butch Cassidy and their "Hole in the Wall Gang." In those days, the area's streets were dotted with saloons and dance halls, which entertained the famous gunslingers.

Neiman-Marcus, Dallas, the first specialty store in Texas, was begun in 1907. Its first owners—Herbert Marcus, his sister Carrie Marcus Neiman, and her husband Al Neiman—brought high-quality merchandise to Texas. Between 1952 and 1979, the store was headed by their relative Stanley Marcus. Under his leadership Neiman-Marcus came to symbolize Texas high-style fashion and luxury.

Caddoan Mounds State Historical Park, near Alto, is a village site of the Caddo tribe, who inhabited East Texas beginning about A.D. 800. It is thought that the Caddoes became extinct because of diseases brought by Europeans. The park covers almost 94 acres and includes two temple mounds, a burial mound, rebuilt dwellings, an information center, and educational hiking trails.

Big Thicket National Preserve, East Texas, called the "biological crossroads of North America," includes 86,000 acres that are home to many different plants and animals. It was made an International Biosphere Reserve by the United Nations (UNESCO). There are eight hiking trails, ranging in length from a half mile to 18 miles, winding through a variety of forest communities that show the Big Thicket's diversity.

Alabama-Coushatta Reservation, Livingston, has been kept since 1854, when Sam Houston requested that the land be set aside for these two Indian groups. A museum displays their culture and history, and summer visitors can also see live performances of dances in traditional costume and an official powwow ceremony.

Lyndon B. Johnson Space Center, Houston, is the mission control center from which U.S. space flights are directed. At the visitor center, a $70 million entertainment and education complex, tourists see displays of spacecraft, historic space equipment, and rocks taken from the moon, as well as videos and interactive multimedia about NASA.

Padre Island National Seashore, the Gulf Coast, is an 80-mile stretch of barrier island noted for sandy beaches, excellent fishing, and its many birds and sea animals. Five miles of the beach are open to camping, and there is an annual festival in mid-November for bird watchers.

The Texas Ranger Hall of Fame and Museum, Waco, presents 150 years of history about the legendary Texas Rangers. On display are old guns and other objects used by the famous law-enforcers.

The State Capitol, Austin, is modeled after the United States Capitol in Washington, D.C., but it is the tallest capitol in the United States. The stately building is made of native pink granite and is surrounded by a tree-studded lawn. There are regular guided tours of the recently restored building and its historic treasures. The Governor's Mansion is across the street.

Elisabet Ney Museum, Austin, is a National Historic Site. In the 1800s it was the home and sculpture studio of one of the state's best-known artists, Elisabet Ney, a native of Germany. Her statues grace the capitol of Texas and the capitol of the United States in Washington, D.C. Many of her sculptures are also on view in the museum.

The Alamo, San Antonio, probably the best-known building in the state, has become a symbol for Texas. During the Texas Revolution, the Mexican army defeated a small group of Texans defending this small fort. It was originally a Spanish mission. Today the Alamo is a museum and shrine in the care of the Daughters of the Republic of Texas. On guided tours, visitors can see actual belongings of rebels who died there, including the famous knife of James Bowie.

Ysleta Mission, El Paso, is Texas's oldest mission, built in 1681–1682 by Tiguas who had been converted to Christianity by Spanish missionaries. It is part of the Tigua Reservation. Visitors today can see the sparkling rebuilt mission with its silver dome, as well as some of the remaining adobe walls of the original building.

Big Bend National Park, West Texas, was established in 1944. It is located in the great bend of the Rio Grande, the international boundary between the United States and Mexico. The park contains 801,163 acres of spectacular mountain and desert scenery, including unusual geological structures and the Chisos Mountains. Campsites are open year round.

FIND OUT MORE

If you want to learn more about Texas, look for the following in your library or video store:

BOOKS:

Bredeson, Carmen. *The Battle of the Alamo.* Brookfield, CT: Millbrook Press, 1996.

Bredeson, Carmen. *The Spindletop Gusher.* Brookfield, CT: Millbrook Press, 1996.

Cummings, Joe. *Texas Handbook.* Chico, CA: Moon Publications, 1992.

Institute of Texan Cultures. *Texans: A Story of Texan Cultures for Young People.* San Antonio, TX: University of Texas Institute of Texan Cultures, 1988.

Ragsdale, Crystal. *Women & Children of the Alamo.* Austin, TX: State House Press, 1994.

Stein, Conrad. *America the Beautiful: Texas.* Chicago, IL: Childrens Press, 1992.

Tolliver, Ruby. *Santa Anna: Patriot or Scoundrel.* Dallas, TX: Hendrick-Long Publisher, 1993.

VIDEOS:

The Alamo. (1966 movie starring John Wayne as Davy Crockett)

For All Mankind. National Geographic. (Clips from Apollo missions, astronaut information)

Lonesome Dove. Cabin Fever Entertainment, 1991.

Texas Rangers: Manhunters of the Old West. A&E Home Video, 1994.

AUDIO TAPES:

De Paola, Tomie. *The Legend of the Bluebonnet.*

Michener, James. *Texas*—read by Peter Graves.

INDEX

Page numbers for illustrations are in boldface.